A Geografunny Guide to the Globe

by Paul Rosenthal

illustrated by Marc Rosenthal

Alfred A. Knopf   New York

To Claudia,
whose confidence and critiques
helped write the book,
and to Malcolm and Maggie,
for whom I wrote it.
P.R.

To Eileen,
whose design holds this book together,
and to Willy, may he always find his way.
M.R.

This book is also dedicated
to Mom and Dad.

OOPS!

THIS IS A BORZOI BOOK PUBLISHED BY ALFRED A. KNOPF, INC.

Text copyright © 1992 by Paul Rosenthal. Illustrations copyright © 1992 by Marc Rosenthal. All rights
reserved under International and Pan-American Copyright Conventions. Published in the United States by Alfred A.
Knopf, Inc., New York, and simultaneously in Canada by Random House of Canada Limited, Toronto. Distributed by
Random House, Inc., New York. Manufactured in the United States of America. 0 9 8 7 6 5 4 3 2 1
Designed by Eileen Rosenthal

Library of Congress Cataloging-in-Publication Data: Rosenthal, Paul. Where on earth: a geografunny guide to the
globe / by Paul Rosenthal; illustrated by Marc Rosenthal. p. cm. Includes index.
Summary: A humorous introduction to various aspects of geography and how they affect life on the
different continents. ISBN 0-679-80833-7 (trade) – ISBN 0-679-90833-1 (lib. bdg.) 1. Geography–Juvenile
literature. [1. Geography.] I. Rosenthal,
Marc, ill. II. Title. G133.R67 1992 910–dc20 92-1227

CONTENTS

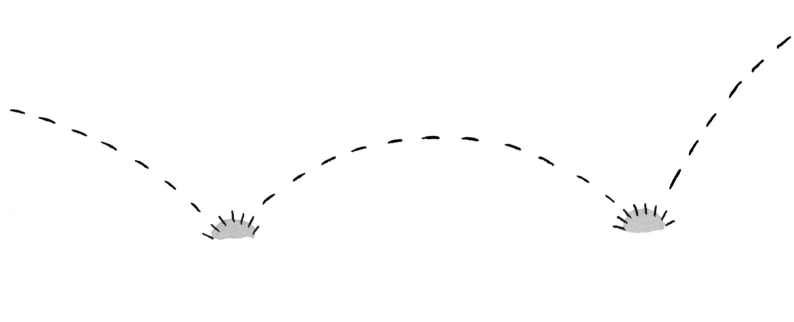

Do you know how to get from your bedroom to your kitchen? Have you learned where your parents' room is? Can you find the bathroom in a hurry?

Of course. They're all part of your home. You certainly know your own home.

The Earth is also your home. It's a little bigger. It's a bit more crowded. And, fortunately, you're not expected to help clean it up after school. Still, the Earth is where you live, and you should know your way around it.

This book is your road map to the planet. It will show you how to go from your bedroom to Bolivia. It will tell you why some places are hot and others are cold, which places have plenty of water and which places are dry, where there are mountains and where there are molehills. It might even help you find a bathroom in a hurry.

More important, it will introduce you to some of the people, plants, and animals that are your neighbors. It will help you discover how geography affects their lives as well as yours—how all of us are shaped by the shape of the Earth.

The Earth is the third planet from the sun, spinning through space somewhere between Mars and Venus. You can recognize it easily by its single moon and by the brilliant blue and green of its oceans and forests.

If you're still having trouble finding the Earth, look down.

When most of us think of our planet, we picture our homes or places we've visited. We imagine an immense stretch of cities or farms or deserts or woods, with a few oceans and lakes scattered about to keep these huge pieces of land from smacking into one another. Yet this image is not accurate. Most of the Earth is under water. In fact, oceans and lakes cover 70 percent of the planet. Land is the exception.

To get some idea of just how wet it is, imagine that the Earth is a bathtub. All the continents and islands put together would be the size of an average six-year-old boy squeezed into one end of the tub with his knees tucked under his chin.

Or imagine that the Earth is a bowl of breakfast cereal. The land would take up about as much room as four round banana slices adrift in all that milk.

In other words, there's a lot of water out there.

The Earth's land area is

4

divided into seven continents. That's easy enough to remember, because important things always come in groups of seven: seven wonders of the world, seven seas, seven dwarfs, and so on.

These seven continents are North America, South America, Europe, Asia, Africa, Australia, and Antarctica.

Antarctica is just a fancy name for the continent around the South Pole. It's pretty empty, except for some

penguins and a handful of scientists. The other continents are filled with plants and animals, people and cities. All are different. And all are the same.

They're different because each continent has its own individual shape, natural wonders, and climate (weather patterns). Each has its own distinctive culture, which includes its traditions, beliefs, and ways of doing things. Each has its own history, its own foods, its own beauty, and its own problems.

But in another sense, the continents are the same, because they're all made up of the same basic rocks and min-

SHARING THE SAME OCEAN...

erals. They're all warmed by the same sun. Most importantly, they're all plugged into the same "ecosystem," which means they all share the same air, the same oceans, and the same winds.

If one country leaves garbage on its beach, that garbage may eventually wash up on somebody else's beach. If one nation fills the air with smoke, that smoke can drift over to a neighboring nation. If one fishing fleet catches all the fish in the sea, then nobody anywhere is ever going to have a tuna salad sandwich again.

This worldwide ecological link is summed up by an old and respected scientific law: "What goes around, comes around."

MOM! CHARLOTTE'S HOGGING ALL THE AIR AGAIN!

...AND THE SAME AIR

Only one Earth, but many continents—all the same and all different! That's what makes the world so interesting and so confusing. Figuring out how these differences and similarities affect us is what geography is all about.

The Continents

Since nobody much lives in Antarctica, nobody will object if we ignore it for now. Let's look at the other six continents first. They can be divided into three groups.

The first group is the Americas. North and South America are separate. But they are connected by a narrow band of land that is called—not surprisingly—Central America.

The second continent group is made up of Europe, Asia, and Africa. These three continents are all bunched together around the Mediterranean Sea. In fact, the name Mediterranean is Latin for "in the middle of the land"—which describes the sea to a T.

If the Mediterranean Sea weren't

there, Europe, Africa, and Asia would be one big landmass. Italy would have to fold up like an accordion to get out of the way. And there would be a lot of extremely unhappy fish.

Even with the Mediterranean there, it's possible to travel from Africa to Asia to Europe entirely by land. Start-

ing out in Egypt (which is tucked into the northeast corner of Africa), hitch a ride on a passing camel and cross the Sinai Desert. That brings you to Israel, which is in Asia. Then take a left and head north through Israel and Lebanon to Turkey, which is mostly in Asia but has a little nubbin sticking into Europe.

The third and final group of continents is not really much of a group, since the only place left is Australia. In fact, for years, people have argued whether Australia is really a continent at all or just an island that got out of hand. But considering how far Australia is from everywhere else, how big it is, and how many Australian animals (such as kangaroos, platypuses, and wombats) aren't found anywhere else, Australia certainly deserves its own category.

Continental Drift

If you get seasick easily, I've got bad news for you. Even when you stay at home in bed, you're actually floating about. All the continents and all the islands on Earth are constantly shifting. It's part of a process called "continental drift."

To understand continental drift, picture the conveyor belt in the supermarket that carries your groceries to the cashier. It comes up out of the counter, moves along toward the cash register, then dives down back into the counter.

The surface of the Earth follows a similar routine. But instead of conveyor belts, it's made up of "plates" formed by melted rock pushing out from deep inside the planet. When the melted rock

reaches the surface, it cools and becomes hard rock (not to be confused with acid rock or heavy metal). As more melted rock muscles its way to the surface and becomes solid, it moves along the surface of the Earth—just as the conveyor belt glides along the checkout counter.

Earth's surface is constantly being rebuilt and reshaped by the bumping of plates. The process is called "plate tectonics" (from *tekton,* a Greek word meaning "builder").

When two plates meet, a number of things can happen. One plate may dive down into the Earth—just as the super-market conveyor belt dives back into the counter.

A head-on collision between plates can pile them up into steep mountains. Or one plate can slide under the other and melt again. Sometimes the melted rock shoots up between the plates and forms a volcano. Elsewhere, side-by-side plates rub against each other and create "faults," which are like cracks in the Earth's crust. Earthquakes are usually a fault's fault.

The various continents and islands, meanwhile, ride atop the plates like groceries riding on the conveyor belt. Except that the continents aren't marked "3 for $1.00."

Don't worry about continental drift shifting everything around, though. You won't notice the changes. The plates are creeping along at about one-third of an inch to six inches a year. At that speed, it will take well over 127 million years before California reaches Japan. It's faster to fly.

It's easy to see that the continents originally fit together before the moving plates pulled them apart. The bump on one continent wedges into the dent on another. This skinny part nestles in that

nook, and some of the bigger islands tuck cozily in between. In fact, you can pretty well take the Earth's landmasses and put them together like a giant jig-saw puzzle.

Sunny Side Up

It's hot in the summer and cold in the winter, right?

Not on the equator. It's always pretty hot there.

The equator is an imaginary circle around the middle of the Earth, halfway between the North and South Poles. If the Earth were a big fat man, the equator would be his belt.

Why is it hot on the equator? To answer that, you've got to understand why there are seasons.

It may seem like up is up and down is down—but life isn't so simple. The Earth is actually tilted on its axis. The axis is an imaginary line running

through the planet like a lollipop stick, with the Earth spinning around it. One end of the axis is called the North Pole, the other is the South Pole. If you face toward the North Pole, you're looking north. South is behind you, west is to your left, and east is to your right.

Since the Earth's axis is tilted, the planet leans, and the sun's light doesn't hit all parts of it evenly.

Now then, Earth is whizzing around the sun. It takes a year to go around once. When the planet is on one side of the sun, the top is tilted away. When it's on the other side of the sun —six months later—the top is tilted toward it.

What does this have to do with seasons? Imagine again that the Earth is a big fat man. You're the sun. If the man leans far forward, his head will be closer to you than his feet. You will still see his belt, but his feet will be hidden behind his big stomach.

If the fat man leans backward, the situation will reverse. You will still see his belt, but this time his head will be hidden from view and his feet will be easy to see.

A similar thing happens to the Earth. When the North Pole is tilted toward

the sun, the warm sunshine hits the northern half most strongly. Less sunshine reaches the south. That makes it summer up north and winter down south. When the North Pole is tilted away from the sun, the situation reverses. That's why the seasons in the Northern Hemisphere and Southern Hemisphere are always opposite (*hemisphere* means "half a ball"—in this case, the Earth).

Spring and fall are the in-between seasons when the Earth is traveling around the sun on its way from one extreme to the other.

Why, then, is the equator warm all year round? Because it is never really in the shade. Just as the belt of the fat man always stayed in view, so the "belt" of the Earth is always in the sun's view.

Which raises an interesting question: If it's always warm on the equator, is it always summer vacation?

The International Date Line

The International Date Line is *not* a telephone number you call to hire an escort for the school dance. It's an imaginary line down the middle of the Pacific Ocean marking where each new day begins.

Before we get hopelessly confused (and it is difficult to discuss the International Date Line without getting hopelessly confused), let's review a few facts about the Earth.

First, Earth is round. Second, it spins on its axis from west to east, making one complete turn every 24 hours. So if you stand in one spot and the sun is directly overhead, it will take 24 hours before the sun is overhead again. That's why each day is 24 hours long.

But for centuries there was no standard way of measuring time. People

figured that when the sun was directly overhead, it was noon, and they set their watches to noon.

As the Earth spins, however, the sun is directly over *different* places at *different* times. So one town might set its clocks five or ten minutes ahead of the town to the west. This became a big problem as travel and communications grew easier and faster. It's awfully hard to make up train schedules when each town along the way is on a different time. And how could cowboys arrange showdowns for high noon if nobody agreed when high noon was?

A clever Canadian named Sir Sandford Fleming came to the rescue. In the

THE INTERNATIONAL DATE LINE IN ACTION!

THESE DRAWINGS SHOW THE EARTH, VIEWED FROM ABOVE THE NORTH POLE...

1870s he divided the planet into 24 zones—one for every hour of the day. Each zone is an hour ahead of the zone to the west of it.

The confusing part comes when you go all the way around the Earth. You cross 24 zones. They span 24 hours—or one full day. Yet you're back at the same time zone where you started.

How can you cross 24 hours and still be back at the time zone where you started? That's where the International Date Line comes in. It separates one day from the next.

The important thing to remember is that the time on either side of the date line is a full day apart *no matter what time it is*. When it's 10 A.M. Thursday on one side of the line, it's 10 A.M. Friday on the other. When it's 8 P.M. Tuesday on one side, it's 8 P.M. Wednesday on the other.

That means if you head west from California to Japan, you jump a day ahead the moment you cross the date line. If you travel east from Japan to California, you go back a day, you don't pass "Go," and you don't collect $200.

... AS IT TURNS, THE DATE LINE SWINGS THROUGH ALL TIMES OF THE DAY.

It's as if you were running laps around the world, and the date line was the starting line. Every time you pass it, you're beginning a new lap. The starting line divides one lap from the next . . . just as the date line divides one day from the next.

The International Date Line runs down the middle of the world's largest ocean—the Pacific. It was put there to avoid dividing any populated areas.

Imagine what would've happened if they *hadn't* avoided populated areas. Imagine if the date line cut through your town. You might leave school Fri-day afternoon, cross the date line on your way home, and it would suddenly be Thursday. The next day would be Friday at your house. You'd get up and go to school, but you'd cross the line going in the other direction. It would be Saturday at the school, and no one would be there.

Fortunately, the date line runs through an ocean. So the only schools it affects are schools of fish.

You can't hear the Horn of Africa, no matter how closely you listen. That's because this particular "horn" is neither a bugle, a tuba, nor a trombone. It's a point of land on Africa's east coast. It is called the Horn because it looks like a sharp horn, jutting into the Indian Ocean and jabbing at Arabia.

It's a breeze to recognize Africa on a map because it is shaped like a zebra's head—and zebras come from Africa. The Horn is the zebra's ear; the Red Sea and Mediterranean Sea form the zebra's mane. South Africa is the zebra's nose. Lake Victoria—the largest lake in Africa—becomes the zebra's eye, staring intently at the nearby island of Madagascar. (Madagascar is certainly worth staring at, particularly if you like lemurs. But we'll talk more about Madagascar later.)

Though Africa is the second largest continent and is nestled close to Europe and Asia (the largest), the peoples of Africa have been relatively isolated until recent times. This was due, in part, to the rugged landscape, which made it hard for outsiders to get inside Africa—and for insiders to get out. Then, too, Africa's coastline is largely made up of rocks and cliffs, with few good parking spaces for ships. That discouraged trade and tourism in many places.

HEY, AFRICA—
WATCH IT WITH
THAT HORN!

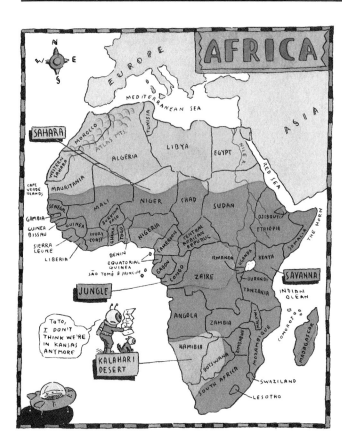

One result of being isolated from outsiders—and from each other—was that local African communities were on their own. Instead of forming big nations with central governments, much of the place remained organized around tribes and families and local chiefs, each with its own customs, laws, religions, and languages, which evolved slowly over many centuries.

In fact, nobody knows exactly how many different African languages there are, but it's probably close to one thousand. That may explain, in part, why the tribes remained separate for so long. Imagine creating a nation where every kid had to learn one thousand languages. Whenever the president said anything, he'd have to say it a thousand times! Everyone would be so busy translating, nobody would have time to do anything.

The difficulty of traveling around Africa and the huge number of tribes and languages have always made it hard for non-Africans to really get to know the place. Even worse, non-Africans have been misled by the movies.

Most films set in Africa show it as one great jungle—a dense tropical forest full of swamps and ferns, with lush green plants, plenty of vines for Tarzan and his friends to swing on, and enough bananas to feed several barrels of monkeys.

These movies are not accurate. Less than a quarter of Africa is forest. The rest is divided between savannas and desert. (A savanna is a grassy plain. A desert is a place with less than ten inches of rain a year . . . all of which usually falls the moment you decide to have a picnic.)

The African desert is warm and dry. Harsh winds often sweep across the flat land. The savannas are also warm, because they're near the equator. But they have rainy seasons, when great storms blow in from the Atlantic and Indian oceans. That's why they're neither deserts nor jungles: there's enough water during the rainy season to grow grass and shrubs, but not enough water year-round to grow forests of trees.

There is some jungle in Africa, but it is confined to a relatively narrow band running east and west across the middle of the continent, where the climate is always hot, humid, and rainy. This lush strip of forest stands out from the rest of the land like a fringe of hair around a bald man's head—the "bald" top being a gigantic desert called "the Sahara."

But unlike a man's head, which keeps getting balder, the Sahara is smaller in

some years, bigger in others. No one knows why Africa's bald spot shrinks now and then—but bald men everywhere would love to learn its secret.

A Hot Time in a Hot Clime

The Sahara is the largest single region of Africa, and the world's largest hot desert. It makes up about one-fourth of the continent.

The name Sahara comes from the Arabic word for "desert." So when we call it the "Sahara Desert," we're actually calling it the "Desert Desert."

The Sahara doesn't have much in the way of water, trees, or people. Though it takes up about as much land as the whole United States, only about two million people live there—fewer than in the city of Chicago.

As we said, the Sahara grows and shrinks from year to year—making it  hard to establish permanent towns along the desert's edge. You're liable to wake up one morning and find that your front lawn has become your front dune.

When folks do find good grassland to settle down on, their livestock promptly eats all the grass and strips the land bare.

People think of hot deserts as mostly sand, like a beach without an ocean. Yet more than 80 percent of the Sahara is not sand but rubble and rock.

Still, plants and animals do manage

to survive. In the desert mountains of the southern Sahara, for example, there are "fog oases"—remarkable areas where a few plants and animals manage to get their water from the fog! That's like you surviving off the aroma of food without actually eating it.

Throughout most of history, the huge Sahara has divided Africa in two. The people of the north stayed in the north, near the Mediterranean Sea. They rarely journeyed south across the Sahara. Who can blame them? It's not much fun to travel through a place that is hot, dusty, has no water, no roads,

and no place to stop for a hamburger and fries along the way.

So instead of going south, the people of the Sahara looked east. They mingled with the Arabs of nearby Asia, just a camel ride away. It was the Arabs who brought the Islamic religion to northern Africa. The desert dwellers also had contact with the Europeans on the other side of the Mediterranean. In fact, in the eighth century, Arab armies that had already swept into the Sahara turned north and invaded Europe (only eight miles away at the western end of the Mediterranean). They liked Spain so much that they decided to hang around and rule the place for seven hundred years.

Because resources are scarce in the Sahara, most of the natives became nomads, or wanderers. That means that instead of settling down in a house or an apartment, they constantly moved from place to place, depending on where they found food and drink. Sort of like rock musicians with sheep.

For their part, the people of sub-Saharan Africa (*sub*-Saharan means "below" the Sahara) were not eager to cross the desert either. In the jungles where they lived, travel was difficult. Nor was there much reason to go anywhere, since there was usually water to drink and fruit and animals to eat. The people below the Sahara generally stayed put.

As for the people of the savannas—the grassy plains—they mixed and mingled more easily. Some were farmers. Some raised cattle—like African cowboys, but without the big hats. Because travel was easier on the plains, many of the tribes did, in fact, unite into large kingdoms. Some of these kingdoms made a good living transporting people and goods across the desert in caravans. (A caravan is a bunch of people traveling together. Wagon trains in America's "Wild West" were caravans.)

Africa's New Old Countries

Many people have trouble remembering all the countries of Africa. One reason is that many of them are fairly recent creations.

This is not to say that there were no African nations until today. Egypt was a superpower three thousand years ago. Carthage, in what is now Libya, was one of ancient Rome's biggest rivals. Music and art thrived in old Africa. American jazz music has its roots in traditional African music. And twentieth-century art, which we call "modern," was strongly influenced by African art, which we call "primitive."

The kingdoms of Ghana, Mali, and Songhai flourished in the open grasslands of Africa well before Columbus sailed to the Americas in 1492. And the great king Shaka ruled the Zulu Empire at the southern tip of Africa before Queen Victoria began ruling the British Empire in 1837.

But most of the old African nations disappeared about 150 years ago. Only recently were they replaced by new nations. It's as if Africa were a giant blackboard, and somebody came along, tried to erase everything that had already been written on it, then wrote something completely new.

What happened? Colonialism happened!

A colony is a land ruled by a foreign country—usually without permission. During the nineteenth century, European soldiers, settlers, and explorers sailed to Africa. They set up governments and built cities and forts.

Great Britain, France, Belgium, Spain, Holland, Germany, Portugal, Italy— these powerful nations divided much of the continent among themselves.

Looking back at those colonies today, we can see that most were not such a terrific idea for the Europeans, let alone for the Africans. It's pretty

expensive to take over a continent that doesn't want to be taken over.

Why, then, did the Europeans do it?

Well, outsiders were accustomed to meddling in Africa. For hundreds of years, African men and women had been captured and sold as slaves in Europe, the Arab lands, and North and South America. This slave trade, one of the cruelest institutions ever devised, may have paved the way for colonialism. Having gotten used to taking Africa's people, it seemed only natural to take Africa's land as well.

Many of the colonists came because they wanted natural riches. Southern Africa, for instance, is chock-full of diamonds and also boasts the world's biggest gold deposits. Other colonies were set up as stopping points along trade routes to India and Asia. And some Europeans came to grow and sell two African plants—coffee and cola—without which the rest of the world would not have had coffee breaks or soda machines.

But much of the rush for colonies was like the rush to carve up the Thanksgiving turkey.

You know what happens on Thanks-

giving. You've piled your plate with candied yams, mashed potatoes, cranberry sauce, and turkey. Apple and pumpkin pies are waiting in the kitchen. Yet still you dive for the drumstick. Why? Not because you're really that hungry, but because you're afraid someone else will get it first.

The same thing happened in Africa. Once one European nation established an African colony, the others panicked. All scrambled for their own bit of

Africa—not because they truly needed it, but because they were afraid that if they waited too long, somebody else would get it first.

The result was that by the twentieth century, the map of Africa didn't tell you very much about the Africans. It just showed which chunk of land was claimed by France, which chunk by Belgium, and so on. These artificial borders rarely matched the natural boundaries of language or culture, so that the colonial nations were often made up of different peoples that didn't particularly want to live together.

The big exception to this was Liberia, the oldest republic in Africa. (A republic is a country not ruled by a king or queen.) Liberia—whose name comes from *liberty*—was established largely by ex-slaves from the United States who returned to Africa between 1820 and 1865. As the only state

below the Sahara that was *never* subjected to colonial rule, Liberia stood

out proudly like a welcome French fry on a plate of Brussels sprouts.

By the 1960s, most colonies had regained their independence. Africa became African again. Today, there are more than fifty African nations. Only thirty years ago, there were fewer than half that number. No wonder people who went to school thirty years ago don't know all the names. You, however, have no excuse!

A Short Trip on a Long River

Africa boasts the longest river in the world: the Nile. The Congo, Niger, and Zambezi rivers are also big. But for all their size, they don't do the Africans that much good. The amount of water carried by all African rivers combined is astonishingly small compared to other continents. If Africa were a swimming pool, you wouldn't want to dive into it.

More important, perhaps, Africa's rivers are full of rapids and waterfalls. This makes commerce difficult. In Europe, Asia, and North America, rivers are used as highways for transporting products and people. Using African

rivers as highways is often like trying to drive down a street full of steps.

How hard is it to navigate African rivers? Consider the Nile. It's the longest river in the world. It has watered the farms of Egypt for thousands of years. And yet, so far as we know, nobody was able to follow it all the way from one end to the other until 1864!

The difficulty of boating in Africa only compounded the travel problems caused by jungles, deserts, and rocky coasts. They all helped keep the continent divided and undeveloped. Trade, science, and industry depend on people being able to get around easily and meet other people. It's like doing the dog paddle: you've got to keep moving or you sink.

Madagascar

Remember Madagascar? It's the island that the zebra seems to be staring at.

Madagascar is an anomaly.

An anomaly is something that seems to defy logic. Cole slaw, for instance, is an anomaly. Why does cole slaw—

which is just chopped-up cabbage—taste good, while plain cabbage tastes like . . . well, like cabbage?

At any rate, Madagascar is an anomaly. The island is less than 500 miles off the coast of Africa. Yet its earliest inhabitants were from Indonesia . . . which is 3,000 miles away on the other side of the Indian Ocean.

It is believed that some time back, perhaps about two thousand years ago, a group of Indonesian sailors lost their way and were blown across to Madagascar, which was then uninhabited.

The animals of Madagascar are also interesting. They probably came from Africa when the island was connected to the mainland. That was a long time ago, though. Many African animals didn't exist when Madagascar was cut off from the mainland—so they never made it over.

For instance, the island is famous for its fifteen different kinds of lemurs, a relative of monkeys and apes. But it has no monkeys or apes. Nor are there lions, elephants, pythons, or lots of other African animals on Madagascar. The island is, however, up to its eye-brows in cows. They were originally brought to Madagascar by people. Now they outnumber the people.

The Animals

No visit to Africa would be complete without mentioning its animals. Elephants and giraffes, zebras and rhinos, lions and leopards, crocodiles, hippos, hyenas, and ostriches come to mind. Yet they hardly scratch the surface of Africa's rich wildlife.

For example, Africa is the winter home of about two billion birds that migrate, or travel, to the vast, warm continent to escape the cold winters of Europe and Central Asia. And that doesn't include the millions more who avoid the bother of migrating and live in Africa year-round. (Why do some birds fly south just for the winter, while others keep warm in Africa year-round? You might as well ask why some people live in Florida and California, and others just come for a two-week holiday.)

Africa also boasts more kinds of freshwater fish and a greater variety of animals with hooves than any other continent. This natural treasure draws tourists from around the globe. Many African nations have set up huge game preserves, where people and animals can look at each other without hurting each other.

One of the continent's more delightful residents is the aardvark. Found only in Africa, the aardvark has something for everyone: the body of a pig, the ears of a rabbit, and the snout of an anteater (though aardvarks do eat ants, they're not members of the anteater family).

Aardvarks grow up to six feet long, nearly as big as a young leopard. Luckily for aardvarks, however, hunters don't like them as much as leopards. Maybe it has something to do with the aardvark's foot-long tongue, which might look silly hanging down a trophy

wall. Perhaps people don't find them pretty enough to kill.

Whatever the reason, it means that the beautiful leopard is now an endangered species, while aardvarks are a dime a dozen.

Have you ever blown up a balloon? Have you ever blown it up too much . . . until it exploded into a dozen little pieces of rubber? If so, you ought to be able to recognize North America.

Like a balloon, North America starts out long and skinny at its southern tip. Like a balloon, it gradually grows bigger and bigger and wider and wider as you head north until, all of a sudden, there's nothing left but a mess of scattered pieces.

Of course, there are differences between North America and a balloon. For one thing, you can't sneak up behind your teacher and pop North America.

The continent stretches all the way from the steamy tropical jungles of Central America to the frozen Arctic, near the North Pole. Most of the people live in between these two extremes, however. They're like Goldilocks.

You recall Goldilocks. She's the kid who waltzed into the Three Bears' apartment without even knocking, then scarfed down a bowl of porridge. In choosing the porridge, her motto was, "Not too hot, not too cold—just right."

Well, the folks who filled up North America have generally followed Goldilocks's example. Most settled down in the "just right" middle rather than the freezing top or steamy bottom.

(Re-)Discovering America

People used to say that Christopher Columbus discovered America. But people were wrong.

Think about it. When Columbus arrived, there were whole tribes on the beach waiting to shake his hand and stamp his passport. Obviously, somebody had already found America. Millions of somebodies, in fact.

DON'T LOOK NOW, BUT I THINK WE'VE BEEN DISCOVERED

HOLLYWOOD PRODUCER?

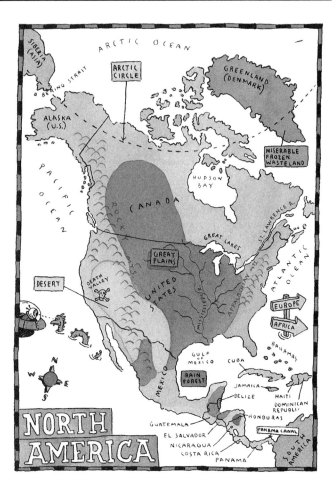

NORTH AMERICA

Columbus called these folks "Indians," because he thought he'd sailed to India. It was an easy mistake to make. How was he to know that someone had left a continent lying around between Europe and Asia?

But the Indians weren't Indians; they were Americans. They probably came to the continent from Asia 20,000 to 30,000 years ago, during the last ice age. Unlike Columbus, they didn't sail across the sea. They walked.

"Walked?" you ask. "Across the Pacific Ocean?"

Yes. But don't you try it without a note from your mom.

Up near the North Pole, America and Asia are only 52 miles apart. The continents are separated by the Bering Strait, with Alaska (in North America) on the east side of the strait and Siberia (in Asia) on the west side. (A strait is a narrow waterway connecting two larger bodies of water—in this case, the Pacific and Arctic oceans.)

How did the Indians walk across the Bering Strait?

During the last ice age, much of the Earth's water was frozen as glaciers or

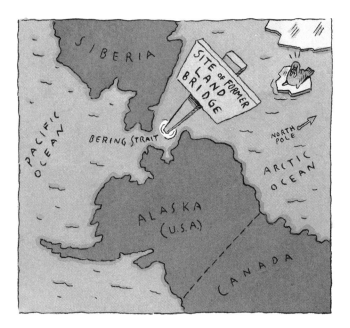

as part of the polar icecaps (the thick, permanent layers of ice at the North and South Poles). This made the oceans nearly 300 feet lower than they are today. The Bering Strait, meanwhile, is only 98 to 164 feet deep. So when the sea level dropped 300 feet, the strait became a dry "land bridge" linking Siberia and Alaska. The ancestors of the Indians toddled across from Asia without even getting their feet wet.

If it had not been for this accident of geography—if the Bering Strait hadn't been so narrow and shallow—America might have remained uninhabited for thousands of years. There would have been nobody for Columbus to call "Indians." No one would have invented the game of lacrosse. No one would have taught the Pilgrims how to grow corn. And instead of playing cowboys and Indians, kids might be playing cowboys and cowboys.

On Your Mark . . .
Get Set . . . Immigrate!

It didn't take long for those who followed Columbus to figure out that America wasn't Asia. They spread the word back home about this nifty new continent, and immigrants started pouring in.

An immigrant is one who moves to a new country. The word is often mixed up with *emigrant*. An emigrant is one who leaves a country. Of course, if you're an immigrant, you're also an emigrant. You can't come *to* some place without going *from* some place . . . unless you walk in a circle and end up back where you started, in which case you might as well have stayed home.

Some who came to America were adventurers, some soldiers, some farmers, servants, bakers, missionaries, and barbers. By the 1600s, Europeans had begun to carve America into colonies, just as they would do in Africa two hundred years later.

Why did immigrants come? Many wanted freedom. They knew that it was easier to "do your own thing" in a big, roomy continent where there were no kings and queens and dukes telling them to keep off the grass.

Some came because they wanted a place of their own. North America had lots of empty space. Europe, by comparison, was more crowded. The best land there was already taken.

Plenty came to America because they were poor. They'd heard that the continent was rich in rivers and resources, that there were acres of fertile farmland, and that all the department stores held terrific Columbus Day sales (limited time only). In a big, undeveloped land, there was plenty to be done, and plenty of cash for those who did it.

Thousands also came because they had no choice—such as the slaves brought from Africa. They too found plenty to do . . . but they didn't get paid for doing it.

The result of all this immigration was a continent full of the old "ha-cha-cha" spirit—the sort of place where you could try anything, say anything, sell anything. North America became a magnet for people who had little or who wanted to get a fresh start.

With all these different folks coming

SOME CAME TO THE NEW WORLD SEEKING FREEDOM... ...OTHERS DID NOT.

to America, the continent became a glorious and varied mixture of peoples. If someone from another galaxy had only an hour or so to visit Earth, North America would be the best place for him to land his saucer. He'd find a sample of nearly every culture, every language, and every type of human on the planet. He'd find restaurants of every description, people of just about every size, shape, and color, and plenty of folks who believed in flying saucers.

The Wide Part of the Continent

Most people who came to North America settled in the wide part of the continent north of Mexico, where there was lots of room for them.

This part of North America is like a giant sofa after your great-aunt Millie has been sitting on it: high on the sides and flat in the middle.

The high sides are mountains. In the East, running up and down the Atlantic coast, are the Appalachians. In the West is a far bigger range: the Rocky Mountains. (That's not a very imaginative name—sort of like calling a place

the Sandy Beach, or the Wet Lake, or the Leafy Forest.)

The Rockies stretch 3,000 miles, from Alaska south through Canada and the western United States nearly to Mexico. They form part of North America's Continental Divide: the steep mountain slopes divide those rivers which flow eastward from those which flow westward.

Between the Rockies and the Appalachians, in the middle of the continent, lie the Great Plains. This is where they grow the "amber waves of grain" you've heard so much about. (We're still looking for the "purple mountain majesties.")

The vast open spaces and cheap ranch land of the Great Plains brought immigrants to the prairie the way a first date brings pimples to a teenager. Cities and towns began breaking out all over the place.

It was here that the cowboy was born. It was here that North America—and the United States in particular—got its reputation as a huge, empty frontier where, with a little brains and a lot of honest sweat, anyone could build a shopping mall.

Of course, the Great Plains aren't all Great. The southwest section is parched desert. No amber waves of grain there, just tumbleweed and scorpions. In eastern California, near the Nevada border, is the hottest, driest part of all: Death Valley. It's the perfect vacation spot—if you happen to be a cactus. Parts of

Death Valley are 282 feet below sea level, which means that if it were near water, it would be under water.

The southwest desert was a natural barrier between the wide part of the continent and the skinnier parts (which we'll check out later). Equally important, the desert climate made southern California dry and sunny . . . perfect for making movies.

The wide part of North America has four wide countries. In order of size, they are: Canada, the United States, Denmark, and Mexico.

"Denmark?" you ask. "Isn't Denmark in Europe?"

Well, yes. But Greenland, which belongs to Denmark, is part of North America.

Greenland, the world's biggest island, is only 16 miles from Canada. The extraordinary thing about Greenland, though, is its name. Green is exactly what it isn't. Most of the island is covered by a permanent sheet of ice about a mile thick.

Why did they name it Greenland? Was it a mistake? If so, some poor Danish mapmaker was probably teased by his friends for years afterward. If it was on purpose, then Greenland is surely the world's biggest practical joke.

What's So Great About the Great Lakes?

There are five lakes in North America that everybody calls "Great." Why?

Well, each of the five is among the largest lakes in the world. Together, they're bigger than any other body of fresh water on Earth. They could more than cover Great Britain. And if they *did* cover Great Britain and the British used the water to make tea, there'd be nearly 2,000,000,000 C.T.B. (cups of tea per Britisher). Imagine the lines at the bathroom around teatime!

The Great Lakes are strung out like stepping stones across the continent. Early immigrants and explorers used the lakes to travel inland. They preferred paddling on water to hacking through the wilderness.

The lakes are connected to the Atlantic Ocean by the St. Lawrence River. People quickly got the bright idea of using this watery highway as . . . well, as a watery highway. From 1783 to 1959, lots of canals were dug to open the way between the lakes and the St. Lawrence River. Today, this network is known as the St. Lawrence Seaway.

Trappers, traders, soldiers, settlers—all sorts of people heading west traveled on the Great Lakes. Others founded cities such as Chicago, Toronto, Green Bay, and Cleveland. They hung around the lakes and built homes . . . which is logical, since the initials of the Great Lakes spell "HOMES"—Huron, Ontario, Michigan, Erie, Superior. (They also spell "SMEHO"—but you try and build a *smeho* in Chicago!)

Of course, the Great Lakes and the St. Lawrence River aren't the only useful waterways in North America. The most famous is the Mississippi, known far and wide as the only river in the world with four *i*'s, four *s*'s, and two *p*'s.

The Mississippi crosses nearly the entire United States from top to bottom.

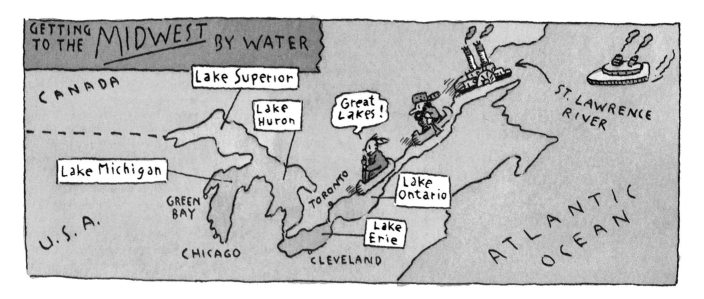

HERE'S A RIDDLE

WHAT HAS
FOUR "i"s
FOUR "S"s AND
TWO "P"s

ANSWER: MISSISSIPPI

On the map, it looks like an enormous tree growing out of the Gulf of Mexico. Its branches are other important rivers that join the Mississippi, creating a transportation network. (A transportation network is like a TV network, except that it carries products instead of programs.)

Unlike Africa, North America is full of places where boats can sail and dock. It has plenty of rivers and the longest coastline of any continent, making it easy for boatloads of immigrants to reach its shores and spread out across the land.

The Narrow Part of the Continent

A long, skinny strip of land dangles off the wide part of the continent like the tail on a kite. This strip is shaped like a chili pepper or a banana—which is handy, since chilies and bananas grow like weeds there. So do weeds. The area is mainly tropical jungle.

This hot property is called Central America, because it's at the center between North America and South America. Seventeen centuries ago, about the time the Roman Empire tripped over its toga and started to fall, the brilliant Maya civilization evolved in Central America. The Maya were great astronomers and mathematicians, and the only North American natives to develop an advanced form of writing. They flourished until the 1500s, when Spanish soldiers known as *"conquistadores"* (conquerors) showed up. "This is Maya land," said the natives. "No," said the *conquistadores,* "it's ours."

Since then, Central America has had a tough time. For many reasons, its countries are generally poorer than their northern neighbors. Central America has few minerals. Much of its soil is not good for farming or grazing. The place is hot, damp, and rugged—all of which were important considerations in the centuries before air conditioners and all-terrain vehicles were invented. And it is a small place with little land to offer. It certainly couldn't compete for immigrants with the wide part of the continent up north.

Sometimes, however, small is better. Being a skinny bit of land made Central America the ideal "shortcut" from east to west. And the shortest cut of all was a place called Panama.

The Panama Canal

To the Central Americans, Central America is home. But to those who

ship stuff around the globe, Central America is a roadblock between the Atlantic and Pacific oceans. More than a century ago, people finally got fed up with sailing the long way 'round the whole continent of South America and decided to dig a canal through the Isthmus of Panama. (An isthmus is a narrow strip of land connecting two larger chunks of land. If you were a continent, your neck would be an isthmus.)

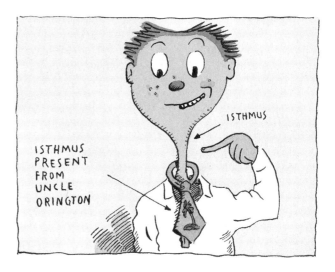

On the map, the project looks easy. At its narrowest point, the isthmus is only 31 miles across. In reality, however, digging the Panama Canal was a pain in the neck (or a pain in the isthmus, if you prefer). Dense tropical forest, heat, malaria, yellow fever, and mosquitoes stood in the way. (Well, the mosquitoes didn't really stand, they buzzed all around. Mosquitoes like to keep busy.)

A French crew began work on the canal in 1880 and gave up ten years later. The United States decided to give it a try in 1904. In 1914 it opened the canal. The new waterway shortened the trip between North America's east and west coasts by 8,000 miles. It was an immediate hit and the Panamanians had a very merry isthmus.

Leave It to Beavers

Beavers helped settle North America.

Beaver hats, beaver coats, beaver ear-muffs—people love beaver fur everywhere except on beavers. Many of North America's earliest explorers were trappers hunting beavers.

Beavers were plentiful. The dams they built helped change streams into meadows—making more land for more beavers growing more fur for more people wanting more beaver coats and hats.

Over time, though, trappers trapped beavers faster than beavers made more beavers. There were fewer beaver dams.

Many wilderness areas suffered—which just proves that nature is like baseball. If you take away one player—the second baseman, for example—the whole game falls apart.

Other North American critters have also been threatened as the land filled up with people, cities, and factories. The bald eagle had a close shave. Only a lot of hard work by a lot of concerned people prevented it from being done in by hunters and pesticides.

And then there's the buffalo.

At one time, an estimated 50 million buffalo roamed. Many Native American tribes depended on them. They ate buffalo meat, wore buffalo leather, slept under buffalo skins, and told buffalo jokes.

But most important, they lived in harmony with the buffalo, hunting only those they needed. The new settlers didn't. They shot buffalo for profit and fun. By the early twentieth century, the 50 million animals had dwindled to about 600. Since then, the animals have been protected by law, and there are almost 40,000 of them today.

The beasts got the last laugh, though . . . because the American buffalo isn't a buffalo at all. It's a bison. The buffalo, found in Africa and Asia, is a different animal entirely. Imagine nearly wiping out an animal and not even getting its name right!

The problems of the bald eagle and the bison show how quickly North America's wildlife and geography have been changed by people. Barely 150

NOW THAT'S WHAT I CALL A GOOD TIME

years ago, the continent was mostly wilderness. The biggest crowds were not on highways and in department stores but around salt licks and water holes. The only skyscrapers were giant sequoias and redwood trees in California.

Today, much of North America is covered by cities, factories, highways, and neatly mowed front lawns. Wilderness areas are preserved in national parks, but they are sometimes as crowded as the cities. The parks are there for people to visit, of course. The problem is that when everyone rushes off to enjoy them, they become less enjoyable. The folks of North America are working hard to balance the needs of people, industry, and Mother Nature.

The nature news is not all bad, however. There are still vast, uncrowded, uncut forests in Canada, acres of woods and grassland in the United States, and unchanged deserts in Mexico. Moose still meander through Maine, coyotes roam Los Angeles suburbs, and bears gawk at tourists in Yellowstone Park. Wild turkeys still survive (they're like the kind you see in stores, only thinner and without the little pop-up device that tells you when they're cooked).

There are plenty of jaguars, parrots, beetles, and snakes in Central America. And the Kodiak bears are still the largest meat-eaters on any continent. You can find them in Alaska—but don't let them find you.

Imagine an ice cream cone. Imagine an ice cream cone with lots of good stuff piled on top—the sort of cone your best friend would make for you, if your best friend worked in an ice cream parlor.

That's what South America looks like.

Fortunately for the South Americans, the place is made of rock, not "rocky road." If it really were ice cream, it would surely melt. That's because South America is more tropical than any other continent: more of it lies near the equator, where the sun beats down most directly.

South America doesn't just look like an ice cream cone. It tastes like one too. Or more accurately, it's a source of the two most popular ice cream flavors: chocolate and vanilla.

Chocolate comes from the cocoa bean, vanilla from the vanilla bean. So the next time your mom says you've got to finish your beans before you get dessert, tell her to give you some cocoa or vanilla. That way you can eat both at the same time.

South America is attached to North America. That's why the two have so much in common, such as Indians who aren't from India, European colonies, immigrants from

around the world, and lots of statues of Christopher Columbus.

As in North America, the European settlers who came to South America described the natives as "primitive." Well, maybe the South Americans hadn't invented a lot of high-tech stuff. But they designed complex irrigation systems and built great cities, roads, and bridges. They crafted exquisite jewelry, excelled at weaving and pottery, and had some excellent recipes for cooking squash.

Besides, who do *you* think was more primitive: the Indians, who drank chocolate and vanilla, or the Europeans, who traipsed around the hot jungle wearing metal helmets and lots of heavy clothes?

But you can't really fault the Europeans for packing the wrong clothes. They weren't sure exactly what they might find in South America. After all, they'd only just learned *how* to find South America. (It's more difficult than you would think, because most of South America is east of North America. It's south, too, of course—but you already guessed that.)

Once one does find the place, it's easy to recognize. The middle is a rich green, as if someone had dipped the ice cream cone–shaped continent in mint

sprinkles. But it isn't mint sprinkles. It's an enormous rain forest called the Amazon.

The Amazon

The Amazon rain forest was named after the Amazons, a group of warrior women who do not live in the Amazon rain forest. (These women are part of an ancient Greek myth about a tribe of fierce females who live without men. The Greeks never explained how the Amazons made more Amazons this way.)

According to local history, the forest was named in 1541 by Francisco de Orellana, a Spanish explorer. The first European to reach the Amazon River, Orellana said that he'd seen women warriors mucking about in the underbrush. For some reason he decided that these ladies must be the legendary Greek Amazons.

Of course, the Amazons could never have gotten all the way there from ancient Greece. Even today, traveling through the dense forest is as difficult and treacherous as pushing onto a bus at rush hour—though, of course, there's no driver shouting "Step to the rear of the Amazon!"

Because it's so hard to get around, most Amazon natives don't. They live in small groups separate from one another. Some tribes haven't changed for centuries. Isolation from each other, from the outside world, and from ancient Greek warrior women has kept many of them in the Stone Age.

Their home is the world's largest, and probably oldest, jungle. It covers about half of South America and accounts for nearly half of the tropical forest on Earth today. Running through the middle of the jungle for nearly 4,000 miles is the Amazon River. Though it's the world's second longest river (after Africa's Nile), it carries far more water than any other. This is probably because it's in a rain forest.

A rain forest is like a bathroom in which someone has left the shower running: humidity and steam, general wetness, damp towels. The Amazon may well be the world's wettest place, except for Beverly Hills, which has so many swimming pools. Out of every five cups of fresh water on Earth, one cup is in the Amazon River and its tributaries. (A tributary is a small river or stream that feeds into a bigger one. If an interstate highway were a river, the on-ramps would be tributaries.)

Three things make the Amazon particularly fascinating. First, it is alive with a staggering variety of plants, animals, insects, and fish.

Second, most of the plants and animals in the forest don't live in the forest. They live *above* it, in the canopy—the cover formed by the treetops.

Millions of monkeys, bugs, plants, and *National Geographic* film crews spend their whole lives in the canopy, a hundred feet off the ground.

Third, the Amazon has what botanists call "crummy soil." (Botanists are scientists who study plants.) Many of the giant trees thrive in only one inch of fertile earth. They stand on tiptoe, with most of their roots above ground.

How do so many plants and animals survive in so fragile an environment? They might ask us the same question.

After all, cities and towns are fragile environments. You can't grow food on a sidewalk. There's no fresh water on a paved street. You can't hunt for meat in suburbia—unless you really enjoy cat burgers and parakeet pie. How do so many people live in such an unnatural environment?

Cooperation. Grocers rely on truck drivers to deliver food. Truck drivers rely on bankers. Bankers rely on electricians. And they all rely on pizza chefs.

Everybody depends on everybody else. Everyone is vital. Take away one group, and the whole system falls apart.

A rain forest is like that too. All sorts of plants and animals and insects work together. Take away one group, and the whole forest falls apart. They all work in concert, turning energy into food.

Energy comes to the forest as sunlight. The giant trees and other plants need sunlight to make food for themselves. The critters living in the treetops get a share of the energy by eating the trees and plants . . . or by eating other critters that eat the plants.

Plants and animals on the ground, meanwhile, wait for fruit, leaves, or dead animals to fall. They eat some of this stuff. The rest rots, becoming part of the soil—where it is "eaten" by the tree roots, which complete the food chain.

Today, this delicate system of cooperation is in danger. Settlers are building roads through the Amazon, turning trees into toothpicks, and trying to use the poor soil as farmland. By the time you're old enough to visit the Amazon, there might not be any Amazon to visit.

Would that matter? Well, nearly half of all prescription medicines in the United States have ingredients made from plants . . . and the Amazon boasts the richest variety of plants on Earth. In destroying the forest, we may already have destroyed some wonder drug or the cure for chicken pox.

If you enjoy breathing, you might also be interested in keeping the Amazon. All plants make oxygen. There's so much shrubbery in the Amazon that it alone may produce up to one-seventh of the Earth's available oxygen supply. So take six breaths. Now take one more. You may have just inhaled a bit of the Amazon.

Not the Amazon

Did you ever meet a kid with really weird hair? Maybe it was dyed green. Or maybe it was all spiky. The point is, you were probably so busy staring at

his scalp that you never noticed the rest of him.

That's South America's problem. The Amazon is big and important, as well as green and spiky. It's so interesting, people often forget to look at the rest of the continent. But the forest is only half the story.

In the southern part of South America is a great grassy stretch called "the pampas." *Pampas* comes from an Indian word meaning "flat surface"—which it is. Like the prairie of North America, this grassland is cattle country. It is filled with gauchos, who are like cowboys, except that a movie about a gaucho would be a "southern" instead of a "western."

Lots of European immigrants came to the pampas. It was certainly easier to make a living there than in the rain forest or the mountains.

Farther south is Patagonia, the largest desert in the Americas. (That's "desert," not "dessert." Remember, South America is not really an ice cream cone.) As you may recall, a desert is a place with little rainfall. Some are hot (like the Sahara), some are not (like Patagonia). Why is there so little rain in Patagonia? Blame the Andes.

The Andes

The Andes are not a bunch of guys named Andy—though it's pronounced that way. The Andes are the world's longest mountain chain. They run the length of the west coast, about 5,500 miles, like a wall between South America and the Pacific Ocean.

How do the Andes make Patagonia dry? Just as a shower curtain blocks water from getting all over the bath-

room floor, the Andes block rain and moist ocean air from getting all over Patagonia.

The Andes also block rivers and streams. Rain falling on the eastern slope is only 100 miles from the Pacific. Yet the water can't flow that short distance west, because the Andes are in the way. Instead, it must flow east to the Atlantic, 2,500 miles away.

The Andes are a wall for people, too, making it tremendously hard to get from the east coast to the west coast. That's probably why there are no countries that span the width of the continent—the exact opposite of North America, where nearly all the countries stretch from the Atlantic to the Pacific.

Living in the Andes isn't easy. Even near the equator, the high mountains make it too cold for much farming, unless you're growing frozen vegetables. The people raise surefooted animals such as sheep, llamas, and alpacas rather than cows, because cows might tumble down the mountains. They'd need "Watch for Falling Cow" signs everywhere. Of course, they'd have a steady supply of milk shakes.

Separated at Birth

South America looks a lot like Africa. This may not be just coincidence. Before continental drift and plate tectonics started shuffling everything around, South America and Africa were attached.

Both continents are wide in the north

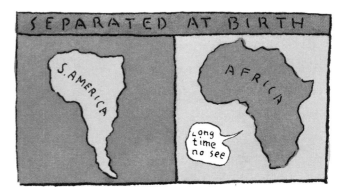

and come to a point in the south. Both have short coastlines, with relatively few of the curves and bumps that make for good harbors.

As in Africa, it's not easy to get around in South America. Walk one way and you bump into the Andes. Another way and the Amazon rain forest is splashing your new shoes. Another way and you come face to face with the Patagonian desert. It's easier to stay home and munch on some cocoa beans.

In Africa, if you remember, difficult travel led to isolated groups of people, each speaking its own language. The same thing happened in South America.

At one time, there may have been as many as 2,000 native South American languages! Even simple communication is impossible with 2,000 languages. If one tribe made a movie, they'd need 1,999 sets of subtitles.

Today, most countries use Spanish and Portuguese, the languages of the European countries that colonized the area. Several hundred Indian languages survive, however . . . particularly in the remote regions, where the people like to gossip about the immigrants without being understood.

Viva Veggies!

Do you like fries and ketchup? Both potatoes and tomatoes come from South America. Avocados? Corn? Pineapples? Thank South America. Ever eat peanut butter and jelly? Peanuts are South American. (Jelly isn't . . . so the rest of the world shouldn't feel too bad.) If you add chocolate and vanilla to the list, you'll see how important South America has been to our bellies.

Another important product of South American greenery is latex, the gooey sap of the local rubber tree. Latex was the original ingredient of chewing gum.

Now it is used in making rubber products such as galoshes, rubber bands, and windshield wipers. If scientists can combine all of latex's remarkable qualities, we might some day have windshield wipers that you can chew or galoshes that blow bubbles.

Fins, Feathers, and Fur

As you'd expect, a continent as diverse as South America—with jungles, mountains, deserts, and plains—has lots of different kinds of animals. There are turtles, seals, sloths, monkeys, jaguars, pumas, and boa constrictors. There are beautifully colored parrots and dull-colored armadillos, toucans (birds with enormous bills) and tapirs (animals with long snouts). There's the condor of the Andes, the world's biggest flying bird, and the penguin of the cold South, which doesn't fly at all.

Llamas, alpacas, and vicunas (like fuzzy camels) are raised for their wool and as pack animals (which means they carry parcels—people actually do all the packing). Guinea pigs were raised by the Indians as food. And Lake Titicaca, high in the Andes, is home to giant frogs up to a foot long. One plate of those frog's legs could feed a family of four.

This rich variety of animal life is good news for the piranhas—small, meat-eating river fish famed for their sharp teeth and healthy appetites. Some kinds of piranha will eat anything that ventures into the water. They are not the only hungry things around, though.

Army ants, traveling in troops of up to a million and a half, devour everything in their path.

But life isn't a bowl of cherries for them, either. South America's giant ant-eater grows up to six feet long . . . big enough to lick a whole brigade of army ants.

Not all of South America's animals are known for what they eat at dinner, however. Some are renowned for what comes out *after* dinner. Every year, more than 350,000 tons of bird droppings—called guano—are collected on islands off the Pacific coasts of Peru and Chile to be sold as fertilizer. That's equal in weight to nearly twelve million ten-year-old kids.

A principal producer of this guano is the booby, a big, awkward-looking seabird. Boobies got their name from people, who thought the birds were stupid—probably because boobies are too easygoing to fuss when another bird steals their food, and because they appear to have a kind of dumb grin on their beaks. One has to wonder, though, who's more of a boob: the birds, or the folks who collect their droppings?

Which of the continent's creatures is the most extraordinary? It's too soon to answer! New kinds are constantly being discovered in the Amazon. Of course, the forest is being chopped down so fast that rare insects, animals, and plants are vanishing every day. South America's most extraordinary inhabitant may be lost before it is found.

ongratulations! You already know every city on the continent of Antarctica.

(There are no cities on the continent of Antarctica.)

You're an expert on the native peoples of Antarctica.

(There are no native peoples of Antarctica.)

You've already learned Antarctica's leading crops, longest rivers, and most popular television show.

(There are no crops, rivers, or television shows in Antarctica.)

Most important of all, you now know that if your teacher says that each kid in the class has to choose one continent to write a report about, and you want to write a really short report, Antarctica is the continent to select.

Antarctica—the land around the South Pole—has almost none of the things most people look for in a continent. It doesn't even really have a name. *Antarctic* means "the opposite of the Arctic"—the Arctic being the area around the North Pole. In other words, the place is defined by what it isn't. It would be like calling North America "Not South America."

Whether Antarctica has any countries is a matter of opinion. Seven nations claim parts of the continent, though they've signed

a treaty agreeing not to do anything about it for now. Argentina, Chile, and Great Britain are particularly insistent. Others, like the United States, don't recognize any claims. Since there aren't any native Antarcticans, the dispute can't be put to a vote.

In short, Antarctica is unlike any other continent. And that makes it fun. It's like coming to school and finding that your teacher is out sick, there's a substitute, and the substitute only speaks ancient Egyptian. You might not like it all the time, but for one day it's kind of neat.

The Deep Freeze

In most places, people talk about the weather to make conversation when they can't think of anything else to talk about. In Antarctica, people talk about the weather because there's a lot of important weather going on.

Let's not beat around the bush: the place is *cold*. About 90 percent of the world's ice is piled up there. This makes Antarctica like a giant air conditioner at the bottom of the world, pumping frigid air to nearby continents and oceans—which is great in summer.

If only Antarctica could be turned off for the winter.

The ice also makes the rugged, mountainous landscape look relatively smooth and flat. It's like when you bake a cake that sticks to the pan and comes out cracked and bumpy. If you smear enough icing on, you can make it look smooth.

Beneath Antarctica's thick icing of glaciers and snow are great mountains and valleys. There are also more than a dozen active volcanoes poking out of the ice and puffing hot air that turns to steam in the chilly skies—just like your hot breath turns to steam on a chilly winter day.

The ice makes it difficult to measure Antarctica or to describe its shape. Every winter, much of the water in the surrounding ocean freezes, filling bays and harbors with ice and making the continent look as if it has doubled in size. In the summer, some of these enormous ice shelves break off and float out to sea as icebergs.

The largest iceberg ever measured floating north from Antarctica was 208 miles long and 60 miles wide—bigger than the state of Massachusetts.

That may explain why getting to Antarctica can be so treacherous, and why no one got close enough to chart the continent until the early 1800s. How would you like to peek out the porthole of your ship and see Massachusetts floating toward you?

Despite all the snow and ice, Antarctica is actually a desert. Rainfall is as rare as a teacher who believes you when you explain that your hamster ate your homework. It's true that there's a lot of snow on the continent, but that's not because it snows frequently. It's just that what little snow does come down each year never melts.

Antarctic Animals

The good news is that you don't need a cat in Antarctica to keep the mice away. There aren't any mice. They can't survive the cold.

The bad news is that nearly all the creatures that can survive in Antarctica are bugs. Mostly mites. Mites are tiny insects. They make dull pets: they're hard to housebreak, and they stubbornly refuse to play with a ball of string. A mite's idea of a good time is sucking the life out of a plant.

There are other invertebrates too, including spiders, lice, fleas, and crustaceans. (An invertebrate has a shell or skeleton on the outside instead of a backbone or internal bones. Sort of like an M&M: hard on the outside, soft inside.)

There's not much in the way of plants, either—mainly lichens, moss, bacteria, molds, yeast, and algae. These generally live near the coast or on the occasional patch of ice-free rock.

The sea around Antarctica, however, is like a watery zoo. It's filled with life. There are vast colonies of plankton—teeny-tiny plants and animals. There are also millions of krill, a shrimpy cousin of the shrimp, about an inch long.

Plankton and krill are favorite foods of seabirds, penguins, seals, fish, squid, and whales. To them, the icy Antarctic sea is like a giant refrigerator where

they come to stuff their faces. (Squid don't really have faces; but whatever it is they stuff, they like to stuff it off Antarctica.)

Most penguins, by the way, don't live on Antarctica. They stay on the warmer islands surrounding the continent, as well as on the nearby southern coasts of Africa, Australia, New Zealand, and South America.

In a way, Antarctica is like a reverse pizza. A pizza has barren crust around the edges and gloppy good stuff in the middle. Antarctica is barren in the middle and full of gloppy good stuff around the edges.

At least, the seals and penguins and whales think it's gloppy good stuff. People are less enthusiastic. Some folks have tried to use this abundant food supply to help feed the world. But shoppers haven't exactly been beating down the supermarket doors searching for krill. Even with coupons.

Besides, if we start eating up this tremendous source of protein, who's going to break the news to the penguins, whales, and seals? They depend on this food. A single blue whale needs up to 5,000 pounds of krill every day. That doesn't leave much for us to share.

"Made in Antarctica"

Antarctica is famous for one product that it exports to the rest of the world: information.

Nearly everyone living on the continent is a research scientist. Nobody knows exactly how many scientists are

there, because their white lab coats blend in with the snow, making them difficult to count. But there are plenty.

Antarctic research blossomed during the International Geophysical Year, a

worldwide scientific extravaganza that lasted from July 1, 1957, to December 31, 1958. (That's actually a year and a half. The scientists were having such a blast that no one wanted to tell them their time was up.)

The Geophysical Year involved 12,000 scientists from 56 nations at 2,500 stations around the globe, all linked by radio. Its purpose was to study the Earth and the factors that affect it. Twelve nations set up 60 research stations in Antarctica during the Geophysical Year. Many of those stations are still operating today.

The scientists found that Antarctica is a great place to study the Earth's past. Just as the freezer in your kitchen preserves food for a long time, so the giant ice sheets around the South Pole preserve rocks, water, and fossils (the hardened remains of ancient plants and animals). And just as in your home freezer, there are lots of surprising things tucked away in the back.

For example, the snow can tell a great deal about the air quality throughout history. How? It's like when your parents make tea. They pour the water over a tea bag. As it drips through, it picks up some of the color and flavor of the tea.

WATER, DRIPPING FROM THE SKY, PICKS UP THE COLOR & FLAVOR OF CHEMICALS, DUST & DIRT IN THE AIR

Water that drips from the sky—as rain or snow—does the same thing. It picks up the color and flavor of chemicals and dirt and dust in the air.

Scientists drill deep holes in glaciers and retrieve samples of snow that fell thousands of years ago. By comparing these to samples taken close to the surface, they can see what the air was like in prehistoric times and more recently. The samples taken close to the surface are invariably dirtier—filled with traces of pollution, fallout from nuclear tests, and bits of the hair spray your aunt Zelda uses.

Not all of the scientists are looking down at the ice, of course. Many of them are also studying the sky. Recently, they've noticed a big hole in the ozone layer over Antarctica.

Ozone is a form of oxygen that blocks deadly ultraviolet light from the sun. A layer of ozone in the upper atmosphere protects us, as if someone smeared the sky with sunscreen lotion to keep the planet from getting sunburned.

Many of the products we use—particularly spray cans and refrigerators—

SAMPLES OF PREHISTORIC AIR

MASTODON BREATH

leak gases that eat away at the ozone layer. That's what's happening over Antarctica. The ozone layer is normally thinner over the North and South Poles anyway, and during the summer, sunlight reacts with these gases to destroy the ozone. The hole closes each winter and reappears each summer . . . a little bigger than the summer before.

It's hard to believe that what we do thousands of miles away affects the sky over the most remote continent . . . but it does. It's like "The Sneeze Felt 'Round the World."

Imagine that a melon salesman in Turkey catches a cold. He sneezes in the direction of a French tourist, who is buying a melon. The Frenchman brings the cold germs back to France and gives the cold to his sister, who sneezes at her boyfriend. The boyfriend goes on a business trip to Japan and, in a crowded conference room, gives the cold to six Japanese businessmen. One of them sneezes at a tourist, who then returns to your hometown and goes to a movie. You sit next to him. He sneezes. You catch the Turkish melon-seller's cold.

Pollution, like a cold virus, can start in a distant place, among people you've never met, and still affect you. The big difference is that covering your mouth when you sneeze won't stop pollution.

Do you know how many aardvarks laid head-to-tail would reach from one end of Asia to the other?

Too many.

Asia is big. Very big. It's got more land, more people, and more kinds of animals and plants than any other continent. It stretches from the Pacific Ocean in the east to the Mediterranean in the west, from the Arctic Sea in the north to the Indian Ocean in the south. Asia boasts the world's highest mountains (the Himalayas), lowest point on Earth (the Dead Sea), biggest lake (Caspian Sea), and stinkiest fruit (the durian).

Nearly one third of all dry land is in Asia. Half the planet's people are Asian. The only thing small about Asia is the word: the largest continent has the shortest name.

Because it's so big, the people, cultures, and land at one end of Asia are very different from those at the other. And those in the middle are different from both.

To cope with these differences, people usually divide Asia into regions, such as the Near East and Far East. The problem with these divisions is that they're European—not Asian. The Near East is only near and the Far East far if you're standing in Europe. To a Japanese person, the Far East is certainly near, and the Near East is pretty darn far.

To further complicate the continent, its western border with Europe is fuzzy. Europe and Asia are both part of one vast chunk of property called "Eurasia." Most geographers consider the Ural Mountains as the dividing line between the two. (A geographer is an expert on geography—as you will be by the end of this book.) But the border between Europe and Asia is based less on geography than on language, culture, and who managed to conquer which piece of real estate.

Let's face it, there's only one way to get the hang of a place as big, lively, and confusing as Asia: visit it.

So hop aboard, we're going for a quick tour. Pack your toothbrush, kiss the cat good-bye, and don't forget to

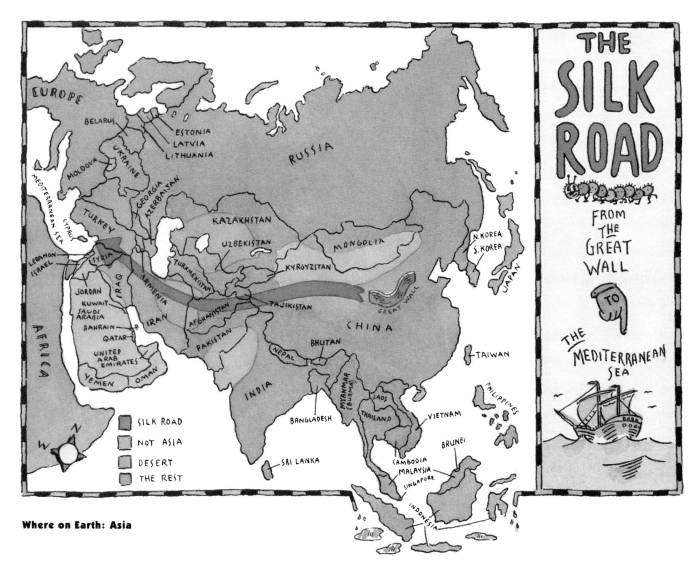

THE SILK ROAD

FROM THE GREAT WALL

TO

THE MEDITERRANEAN SEA

SILK ROAD
NOT ASIA
DESERT
THE REST

bring your chopsticks. We're going to get the lay of the land with a 4,000-mile journey across the middle of Asia along the Silk Road.

The Silk Road

The Silk Road is not a street made of cloth. It doesn't have "Dry-clean Only" written on it. It isn't even really a road. There are no signs saying "Silk Road, Next 3 Exits."

If it's not a real road, how can you travel along it? Think of geese.

When geese head south for the winter, they don't drive along a highway (though they do honk a lot). Yet all the geese head in the same direction and follow the same general route year after year.

The Silk Road is similar—a route that people have followed year after year. For centuries, traders and merchants have traveled back and forth between China and Europe. Many of the great trading cities of the ancient world, places like Samarkand and Tashkent, Baghdad and Damascus, sprang up along the route, providing markets and inns for people, and pit stops for horses and camels.

Lots of different goods—and ideas—traveled back and forth along the Silk Road. The most famous product, of course, was silk. For centuries, only the Chinese knew the secret of producing that exquisite cloth. So when a Roman emperor bought a new silk toga or, a thousand years later, a French knight opened the visor on his armor and sneezed into a silk hanky, the toga and

hanky had traveled 4,000 miles along the Silk Road.

The Silk Road begins in central China. It runs westward along part of the Great Wall of China, which is the biggest human-made structure on Earth (not including Belinda, the circus fat lady). The Chinese began building the 1,500-mile-long wall more than two thousand years ago to shield themselves from the fierce warrior tribes who wandered about Central Asia robbing, burning cities, and saying "Sez you" a lot.

The idea behind the Great Wall was simple. In the north, stretching across the plains of Mongolia, the huge, windswept Gobi Desert prevented invaders

from sneaking around that end of the Wall. In the south, the equally treacherous Takla Makan Desert stopped them from slipping around the other end. As long as the Chinese remembered not to answer the Great Doorbell on the Great Door in the Great Wall, everything was dandy.

The only safe route between the heart of China and the West was along the Silk Road. After leaving the Great Wall, the Silk Road squeezed between the two deserts and then skirted around the foothills of the Pamir Mountains. The Pamirs are one of several mountain chains bunched together in the middle of Asia, like the hump on the back of a camel. These chains include the Himalayas and other mountains that are hard to cross and even harder to spell.

Continuing west from the Pamirs, the

Silk Road crosses the fairly flat, dry land that is now Iran, Iraq, and Syria. It ends at the Mediterranean Sea, a short boat ride from Europe and North Africa.

All told, it was a long, dusty, difficult journey, across deserts, over hills, and around mountains. You can understand why Christopher Columbus and others were eager to find a simple way of reaching China by sea.

Of course, it was rare that anyone actually traveled the whole length of the Silk Road. Instead, products were passed along from one person to the next, like a good joke.

Now that we've finished our journey, let's go back and look at some of the different regions more closely.

All the Tea in China

Legend says that in 2737 B.C., Chinese emperor Shennong came up with the idea of making tea. "We've got all these blasted teapots lying around," he said (in Chinese). "We might as well put something in 'em."

Today, Emperor Shennong is long gone. But people everywhere still drink tea. And that's only one of China's last-

ing contributions to the world. In addition to figuring out how to make silk, this great nation at the eastern end of Asia also invented gunpowder, fireworks, paper money, and pork fried rice.

China's early growth owed a lot to geography. Flat plains and navigable rivers along the coast and in the middle simplified travel and trade. Rich soil and plenty of water for irrigation helped the ancient Chinese settle down and build a strong agricultural economy. (Agriculture is a fancy name for

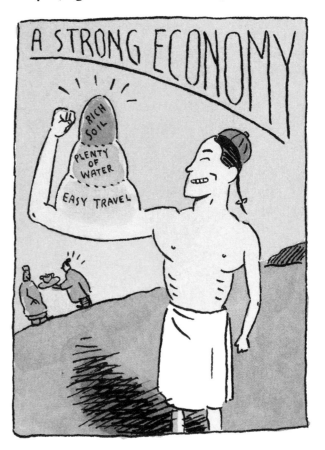

farming.) A long seacoast gave them a steady supply of fish sticks.

Over the centuries, much of eastern Asia was dominated by the Chinese Empire. (An empire is like a kingdom, only bigger. Empires are like umpires. Both tell others what to do.)

Korea (in the north) and Vietnam (in the south) were once ruled by China. Japan (offshore to the east) uses the Chinese writing system. In Singapore (far south of China), they speak Chinese. Chinese merchants set up shops across Southeast Asia in Malay-

sia, Cambodia, the Philippines, Indonesia, and elsewhere.

Today, China has more people than any other country. One out of every five people on Earth is in China.

Siberia

When Russia was an empire, its emperor called himself a "tsar." Others sometimes called him a blockhead. Those people were sent to Siberia.

Siberia was where tsars put prisoners. It's a big, empty, cold place, just above China, covering the whole northern stretch of Asia.

Lower Siberia is a flat plain. Middle Siberia is mainly forest. Upper Siberia is in the Arctic, where the most popular sport is rubbing your nose to keep it from freezing off.

The native Siberians are related to the Indians of North America, who crossed from Siberia to Alaska. There aren't many native Siberians, though. The remote region is not an easy place to live in. (If it were a comfy spot, do you think the tsars would have sent prisoners there?)

Recently, Siberia has been developed by Russia for lumber, coal, oil, and

natural gas. Traditional occupations include reindeer herding, fur trapping, and writing a hundred times on the blackboard: "The tsar is *not* a block-head."

The Steppes

There are no steps in the Steppes. They are as flat as a high school orchestra.

The Steppes are a huge, treeless plain on the southern edge of Siberia. The name comes from a Russian word meaning "huge, treeless plain on the southern edge of Siberia."

(Sometimes, huge, treeless plains in other places are also called steppes because they remind folks of the one on the southern edge of Siberia—and because it's a lot easier to say steppe than "huge, treeless plain.")

The Steppes run most of the way across Asia, from China and Mongolia right up to Hungary, in the center of Europe. There is not enough rain on the Steppes to grow thick forests. But there is enough rain for grass. Miles of grass—which makes it a perfect place to raise sheep. The nomadic peoples of the Steppes follow their woolly flocks across the grassland (a sheep's idea of heaven), stopping each night to set up camp and cook lamb chops (a sheep's idea of hell).

The flat, open Steppes are a natural highway between East and West. Much of the Silk Road runs along the Steppes. So too have dozens of armies. The fabled trading cities and marketplaces of Central Asia are on the Steppes.

This continuous parade of merchants and warriors has made the Steppes a patchwork quilt of peoples—Mongols, Chinese, Tibetans, Armenians, Turks, Iranians, Afghans, Georgians, Kurds, Uzbeks, Indians, Ukrainians, Russians, and dozens of others.

With its markets full of rugs, cloth, spices, crafts, and food, the Steppes were the shopping mall of the ancient world: a convenient place to buy, to hang out, and to launch an invasion.

The REAL India

You'll remember that when Christopher Columbus landed in America, he thought he was in India. That's why he named the American Indians Indians, even though they weren't.

Well, in India, the Indians are indeed Indians.

India and its neighbors Pakistan and Bangladesh are on a great, triangular wedge of land known as the Indian subcontinent (as we said, "sub" means below—in this case below the rank of a continent). The subcontinent dangles off the underside of Asia. About 100 million years ago, it was an island. As plate tectonics moved the continents around, the triangular landmass smacked into southern Asia. After millions of years of being squeezed by Asia and the subcontinent, the land between them folded up like an accordion. These folds are the Himalayas, the world's tallest mountains.

The Himalayas separate India from China. Sandwiched in between are the countries of Nepal, Sikkim, and Bhutan. Some people believe these mountains are home to the Abominable Snowman, who is sort of like Frosty with a chip on his shoulder.

The Indian subcontinent is cut off

THE BIRTH OF THE HIMALAYAS

WATCH OUT FOR SOUTHERN ASIA!

from Asia on the east and west by water, and along most of the north by the Himalayas. This isolation has had two opposite effects.

First, it made the region a lively mix of different peoples. Every time invading soldiers marched east or west across Asia, some of them were stopped by the mountains or shores of India. Many settled down and bought a little house with a white picket fence and an elephant curled up on the hearth. Today, India has sixteen official languages and hundreds of dialects, or local variations on these languages. Just flipping around the TV dial can be like visiting the United Nations.

Yet isolation has also united these varied peoples. Living together, apart from the rest of Asia, gave them much in common.

India's separateness from Asia let the subcontinent come up with a distinctive culture that has influenced many of its neighbors. Buddhism, from India, became the major religion in China, Tibet, Thailand, and far-off Korea and Japan. Hinduism, an even older Indian religion, spread to parts of Indonesia and Nepal. Even rice, the world's most widely eaten grain, probably came from India.

BUDDHISM HINDUISM RICE

INDIA DO NOT DISTURB

WHAT'S GOING ON IN THERE?

CURRY

For centuries, European nations were interested in India. Jutting into the Indian Ocean, halfway across Asia, India was a logical stop for ships sailing east and west. In addition, European chefs had prized Indian spices since the days of ancient Rome. And why not? What's the use of being a big, fancy world power if all your food tastes like something from the school cafeteria?

In the nineteenth century, Great Britain succeeded in turning most of India into a colony. They hung on to it until 1947. Not that the prized Indian spices helped the British much. They were still jeered as having the worst food in Europe—nothing but kidney pudding, boiled parsnips, and oatmeal.

The Land of Sand

Take some sand. Add heat, belly dancers, and palm trees, and what do you get?

Well, yes . . . you do get the beach in California. But you also get Arabia. Or at least, you get the Arabia we've all seen in the movies. The Hollywood image is partly accurate. The place is indeed dry and sandy. People do ride camels, and some women do bare their

bellies and go dancing cheek-to-sheik.

It's true that big hunks of the area are empty desert where, on Saturday nights, the only date you can get has a pit in it. But southwestern Asia is more varied than that. Some parts border the Mediterranean Sea and the Tigris and Euphrates rivers. This lush section, called "the Fertile Crescent," is a crescent-moon–shaped area with enough water for crops and people.

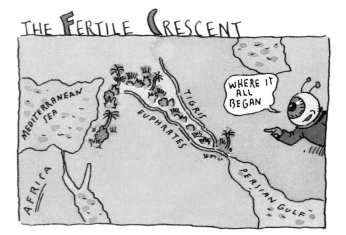

Some scholars think that human civilization was born in the Fertile Crescent—that this is where ancient men and women first got the idea of settling down as farmers rather than traipsing around the countryside in search of food, like prehistoric teenagers out raiding a giant fridge.

Other scholars disagree, insisting that civilization began much later with the invention of napkins. In any event, lots of ancient cultures flowered in the Fertile Crescent. The Persians, Babylonians, Hebrews, Sumerians, Assyrians, Philistines, Turks, and others all pitched tents there at one time or other.

Much of their success was built on trade. In fact, this part of western Asia is often called the Middle East, because it's in the middle between Europe and the rest of Asia. Any merchant commuting between East and West has to pass through here. If Asia were a subway, the Middle East would be its turnstile.

The region is also famous for some local products. Its biggest export used to be its three native religions: Judaism, Christianity, and Islam. Today, southwestern Asia is better known for another export. Can you guess what it is? You probably have some in your family's car.

No . . . *not* fuzzy dice. Oil! The deserts around Arabia and the Persian Gulf hold about one-third of all the Earth's oil. Its great underground reservoirs of oil were first discovered in the 1930s and 1940s. The area hasn't been the same since. It's a great example of how geography affects folks. What was once a poor desert land with few people is now a rich desert land with few people. Air-conditioned office buildings rise where tents once stood, and even

the camels drive their own cars now.

Of course, oil and wealth have brought problems, too. It's difficult to change people overnight from shepherds, craftworkers, and merchants into bankers, computer programmers, and engineers. And of course, having something that everyone else wants—like oil—means having something that must be protected.

Plants and Animals in Asia

Let's not talk about plants and animals in Asia. It's too big a job. It was tough enough covering all the regions of the huge continent. How are we supposed to cover all the beasts and greenery in a place where people ride camels in the desert and horses on the Steppes, where they use elephants as forklifts in India and drink yak milk in Mongolia?

How can we do justice to the bears, wolves, reindeer, sable, cattle, peacocks, monkeys, oxen, pigs, panthers, pandas, rhinos, water buffalos, tigers, and the thousands of other Asian natives?

As for plants, one could write a whole book on nothing but three of Asia's grains: wheat, soybeans, and rice.

To get some idea of how important these grains are to us, imagine a world without wheat. There'd be no bread, cookies, or pizza dough. You'd have to eat the cheese and pepperoni right off the plate. As for soybeans, consider Chinese food without soy sauce. And with no rice to throw at weddings, there'd be nothing to do but stand around talking to Uncle Warren (the one who still thinks it's funny to pre-

THE ANIMALS WE ARE NOT TALKING ABOUT...

I DIDN'T WANT TO BE IN THAT STUPID BOOK ANYWAY...

PERHAPS 'TIS ALL FOR THE BEST.

HMPH!

MIGHT AS WELL GO HOME

tend he's taking coins out of your ear).

No . . . not enough time. Besides, it's late. We're all tired.

Let's just look at something fun. Let's look at the durian.

The durian is a round fruit, about six to eight inches across. It's grown in the tropics of Southeast Asia (below China).

The soft, custard-like flesh of the durian is famous for its flavor and aroma. Some say it's the best-tasting fruit in the world. Everyone agrees it's absolutely the worst-smelling.

❧ *THE DURIAN*
The nose and the mouth can't agree
On the durian, a very strange fruit.
It tastes just as good as could be.
It smells like a sweaty old boot.

Okay. That's enough about Asia. Let's break for lunch.

A cracker is flat and dry. Australia is flat and dry.

Australia is not, however, a cracker. So the next time you're looking for a cracker on which to smear peanut butter, make sure you haven't gotten Australia by mistake. Try saying "Howdy, mate," or "G'day," or one of the other things that Australians are famous for saying. If there's no answer, go ahead and smear. It's a cracker.

The smallest of the seven continents, Australia is nestled in between the South Pacific Ocean and the Indian Ocean. It is directly south of Indonesia and Japan.

The continent of Australia has only one country on it (which is also called Australia) and one official language (English—though some native peoples speak their own languages). This saves a lot of time and trouble and prevents fights. You can't go to war with your neighbors if you haven't got any.

It also lets the people concentrate on

Australia

A cracker

building cities, barbecuing shrimp, and doing other useful things instead of arguing about borders and such. And think of all the money Australians save by not having to make thousands of highway signs saying "Welcome to Australia."

The name Australia means "southern place" (*auster* is Latin for "south"). People sometimes call it "down under" because, to a European or an American looking at a globe, Australia is tucked in down under the equator. Of course, to Australians, the rest of the world is "up over."

As we've already established, Australia is flat and dry. About one-third of the land is desert. Another third is semi-desert grassland, similar to the Asian Steppes. And like a steppe, this plain has become a giant restaurant for sheep and cattle.

If you're looking for water and greenery, head toward the beaches. Everyone else has. Most of Australia's people and cities are crowded around the continent's coastline.

That's another difference between Australia and a cracker, by the way. When you put stuff on a cracker, you usually pile it up in the middle and leave a little empty space around the edge. In Australia, everyone is piled up along the edge. There's lots of empty space in the middle. Australians call this empty middle the Outback.

The Outback

The Outback is a big, dusty, dry expanse of kangaroo-colored land. There are no full-time rivers in the Outback. When it rains, the rivers become great rushing torrents. When the rain stops, they dry out—sometimes for years at a time.

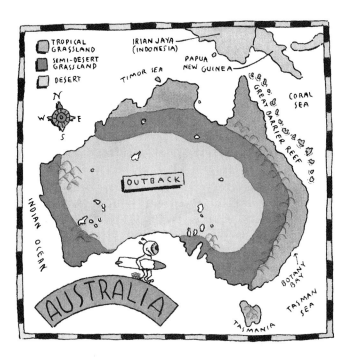

Most of the lakes in the Outback aren't much wetter. Many of them are salt beds for most of the year: areas where there was once salt water, but the water has since dried up. A big storm will flood them—but only for a while.

All this makes it tough to draw accurate maps of the Outback. It also means that the rivers and lakes aren't very useful. You can't very well load your boats with products and passengers, then sit around waiting for rain. But it can lead to some interesting

weather reports—"Cloudy, with a chance of rivers."

The Australians make the best of it, however. Along the Todd River, for instance, in the town of Alice Springs, they hold an annual boat race called "Henley on the Todd," named after the Henley Regatta boat race in England. The river is usually dry, but the Australians don't let that get in the way of a good race—the boats are carried by runners.

The harsh Outback has shaped the Australian people and society in many ways. For one thing, it has kept most folks crowded along the more comfortable coastline, busily saying "G'day" and "Howdy, mate" to one another. As for those who do live in the Outback, the struggle for survival has made them

independent, self-reliant, and great at carrying boats.

In many ways, Australia's Outback is like North America's "Wild West." Both are immense prairies where people raise cattle and sheep. Both are rugged lands that attracted rugged people. And both were obstacles in the way of folks moving from one side of the country to the other.

In North America, the invention of the railroad helped overcome this obstacle. You didn't have to be a hotshot cowboy or brave pioneer to buy a train ticket. In Australia, taking a train cross-country wasn't so simple, because each of the Australian states built different-size railroad tracks.

More recently, cars and airplanes have made travel easier. Highways cross the plains, and since 1928 doctors in the Outback have used airplanes to make house calls. On some of the biggest ranches (which Australians call sta-

tions), the ranchers ride planes instead of horses to herd cattle. This has advantages and disadvantages. It's nearly impossible to rope a steer from the air . . . but you don't have to watch where you put your boots.

The Australians

Australia, like the Americas, was colonized by Europeans. And as in America, there were native peoples who lived, worked, and played hopscotch there long before the Europeans arrived. In Australia, these original citizens are known as aborigines. (*Aborigine* means the first people to live in a place.)

The aborigines probably came from Asia. Flip back to the map of Asia on page 60. You'll see that Southeast Asia dangles down in a long, skinny arm of land, then breaks up into the islands of Indonesia. These islands stretch 1,000 miles toward Australia like a line of stepping stones.

If that map had been drawn 30,000 years ago, during the last ice age, it would look a lot different. For one thing, the paper would be yellowed and torn by now. For another thing, there'd be less ocean, because lots of seawater was frozen as part of glaciers and at the North and South Poles. With the ocean level lower, the ground between the Indonesian islands would have been left high and dry, forming a land bridge between Asia and Australia.

A bunch of Asians probably walked south along this dry path to look around. Eventually, the glaciers melted and the seas rose. The land bridge disappeared, and the people discovered that instead of being visitors in Australia, they were now aborigines. The same thing happened in North America, you'll recall, when the Indians walked from Siberia to Alaska. You've got to watch out for those land bridges.

The aborigines were hunter-gatherers. This means that instead of settling down to grow rutabagas and raise pigs, they puttered around the countryside looking for animals to hunt and plants to gather.

Hunter-gathering may seem like fun,

but it's not always easy. Hunter-gatherers have little control over much of their lives. Their moms never ask, "What do you want for dinner?" They have to eat whatever wanders by.

Of course, hunter-gatherers are more in harmony with the environment than are farmers. They're like the American Indians who, you may remember, hunted buffalo (bison!) for meat and leather but did not destroy the great herds. Similarly, Australian aborigines used what they found and left the rest alone. That's why they were able to live in Australia for 30,000 years without changing it much.

That ended when the Europeans arrived. The first to land, in the early 1600s, were the Dutch, who named the land New Holland. The British soon took over, however. In 1770, the English explorer Captain Cook popped in to see what was cooking.

The bay in which Cook parked his ship was full of interesting new kinds of plants worth studying. He thought of naming the place "Interesting Plants Worth Studying Bay," but the name

didn't fit on his map. Instead he called it Botany Bay, since botany is the study of plants . . . and is only six letters long.

Eighteen years later, in 1788, Great Britain began colonizing the distant continent. Not far from Botany Bay they found one of the greatest natural ports in the world and named it Sydney.

The British came to Australia for lots of reasons. Its harbors and location made it a convenient trading base for nearby East Asia and the South Pacific.

Also, King George wanted to make up for the loss five years earlier of the American colonies, which told Great Britain to take a hike in 1776 and finally won their independence in 1783. It's like when somebody snatches a kid's toy in the playground, and his mom quickly shoves a new toy into his hands to keep him from crying. Australia was King George's new toy.

Another reason was that the British

jails were full. Someone remembered there was a big, empty continent just lying around gathering dust and suggested sending convicts there. The king thought that was a spiffy idea, and for nearly a century—up until the 1860s—British prisoners were transported to Australia. Today, the great-grandchildren of those prisoners are citizens in good standing.

Once the colony was established, immigrants began coming from Great Britain, Ireland, and across Europe. Each had his or her own reasons. Some came because they were poor and wanted to start a new life. Some came

because gold was discovered in Australia in 1851. Some came because they liked those nifty Australian hats with the brim folded up on one side. And today, many come from around the globe because Australia is a stable, prosperous democracy.

As in North America, immigrants vastly outnumber Australia's native peoples. Just as America's Indians were put on reservations, so were many of Australia's aborigines. And Australia, like North America, is a vivid example of how the environment has been reshaped by humans.

The colonists cleared land for farms and homes. They planted European and American plants. They built cities, factories, highways, and railroads. And perhaps more important, they brought new animals.

Animals—Old and New

Remember Dorothy? She got blown "over the rainbow" to the Land of Oz. If she'd been blown "down under" the rainbow instead, she would have found herself in the "Land of Ah's." That's because Australia is chock-a-block with cute animals . . . the kind that make you smile and go "Ahhh!" when you see them.

Australia is the home of kangaroos (ahhh), koala bears (ahhh), wallabies (ahhh), and emus (ahhh-ahhh-ahhh-choo! I'm allergic to emus). It's famous for unusual plants and animals, many of which are unlike the plants and animals found anywhere else. This is largely a result of Australia's isolation.

We said before that Australia was like a cracker. Well, if it really were a

cracker, it would be the one that inevitably slips off the snack plate and gets lost behind the sofa. For thousands of years, Australia was cut off from the other continents. Its shrubbery and wildlife were left alone to do their own things . . . to which the marsupials cried "Hot diggity!"

Marsupials are primitive mammals. Like other mammals, they have hair or fur, make milk to feed their young, and give birth to live babies instead of laying eggs. But marsupial babies are born too early to go it alone. They take one glimpse of the world outside, shout "Yikes!" and skedaddle into a special pouch on the mother marsupial. Then they lie low for months until they're big enough to come out and play.

There are no marsupials in Europe, Africa, or mainland Asia. Only two families of marsupials live in the Americas: the opossums, which are found all over the place, and South America's "marsupial rats," which look like (guess what!) rats.

In Australia, however, you can't turn around without tripping over a marsupial. The most famous are the kangaroos. There are nearly fifty species of them. Some kangaroos are as tall as a basketball player and can jump 30 feet. If you could just get them to wear shorts and teach them to dribble, your team would be unbeatable.

Sorry, no Marsupials in Europe.

Australia is also home to monotremes. These confusing mammals have hair and make milk—but they lay eggs like reptiles. There are three kinds of monotremes. Two of them, the short-nosed and long-nosed echidnas, eat ants, which makes them useful to have along on a picnic. The third is the platypus, which is a zoo unto itself. It has the broad bill and webbed feet of a duck, the soft fur and flat tail of a beaver, and the enormous appetite of a professional wrestler.

For thousands of years, Australia's marsupials and monotremes were happy as clams. (Clams may not actually be all that happy, but they don't complain much.) Then the Europeans showed up with a whole variety of mammals. These imported animals upset the natural balance.

How can a few mammals cause trouble? You never know what might happen when you start changing things. Suppose a kid gets a dog. The dog chases his cat away. With the cat gone, the mice come out and scare his baby sister, who drops a glass of tomato juice all over the white sofa. Outside, meanwhile, the cat starts hunting birds. Fewer birds means more worms. More worms makes the kid think of fishing. Who could've predicted that getting a dog would mean fewer fish and more stains on the sofa?

One European animal proved especially destructive. The rabbit. A few escaped from one farm. They immediately started doing what rabbits do best: making more rabbits. Within fifty years, they'd spread across Australia, devastating crops and grassland like an army of cottontailed lawnmowers.

MOST DESTRUCTIVE ANIMAL

Cows and sheep also changed Australia, eating up acres of prairie grass that used to feed kangaroos. The kangaroos were hopping mad.

Like the aborigines, many of Australia's animals have been shoved aside by a stampede of immigrants.

Tasmania and the Great Barrier Reef

Two of the best-known places in Australia aren't actually in Australia. One is Tasmania. The other is the Great Barrier Reef.

Tasmania, a small, heart-shaped island just off the southeast coast of Australia, is one of Australia's seven states. It's only about 150 miles offshore. Yet it is about as different from Australia as cream pie is from creamed spinach. Australia is relatively flat; Tasmania is mountainous. Australia's weather tends to be hot; Tasmania's tends to be mild. Australia is dry; Tasmania has two major river systems and more than four thousand lakes. Tasmania also has the famous Tasmanian devils—which is not a football team but a nasty-tempered marsupial with a "devilish" expression, like someone who has just smelled a ripe durian.

Australia's other offshore marvel is the Great Barrier Reef, the biggest structure ever built by any living creature.

The Great Barrier Reef is a network of thousands of coral reefs. Coral are tiny sea animals. The young ones live atop the skeletons of their parents. (We don't suggest you try this at home.)

Over time, skeletons keep piling up into underwater mountains, with a thin layer of living coral on the top. In the

Great Barrier Reef, the coral mountains are so high that parts of the reef stick out of the water at low tide.

The reef runs along the northeast coast of Australia for roughly 1,250 miles. That's about the same length as the entire west coast of the United States, from Mexico to Canada.

Captain Cook discovered the barrier reef in 1770, and probably wished he hadn't. His ship *Endeavour* ran aground on it during the night.

Among the more astonishing inhabitants of the Great Barrier Reef are the giant clams. They can grow up to four feet wide and weigh up to 200 pounds. One giant clam would yield enough clam chowder to make 800 hungry people as happy as a platypus.

French toast. Spanish omelets. Hungarian goulash. Swiss cheese. Irish stew. Greek salad. Dutch cocoa. Scotch broth. Italian ices. Turkish coffee. Belgian waffles. Polish sausages. German pancakes. Welsh rabbit. Russian dressing. Swedish meatballs. English muffins. Prune danish.

Ever notice how many European countries are known for their food? Even cities are famed for good eats: Viennese pastry, Parma ham, Bologna (which we call baloney), chicken Kiev . . . not to mention certain fast foods from Hamburg and Frankfurt.

Europe has contributed more to the world than calories, of course. Without

European writers such as William Shakespeare, Beatrix Potter, and P. G. Wodehouse, your local library would be empty enough to use as a bowling alley. European musicians, including Mozart, Tchaikovsky, the Beatles, and Beethoven, are heard around the globe. Its artists, from Michelangelo and Rembrandt to Picasso and John Tenniel (who illustrated *Alice in Wonderland*), have enriched the world as much as Europe's great chefs. And this list doesn't include all those clever ancient Romans and Greeks.

These achievements in food, literature, and art are evidence that Europe is a user-friendly continent. The climate is mostly mild, the soil fertile. There are good harbors and navigable rivers. Europe is the only continent with no deserts. Its mountains aren't *so* big that they get in everyone's way. Europeans have plenty of minerals and water. And think of the money they save on European vacations! All in all, Europe's cooperative geography has left its people plenty of spare time to invent cream puffs and write poems about daffodils.

This is not to say, of course, that every inch of Europe is a park, that there's never a drought or a heat wave, and that the people lounge around the house all day eating bonbons and playing dominoes. On the whole, however, Europe is lucky to be where it is.

But where is it?

Where Is Europe?

If Asia were a face, Europe would be its nose. (Let's hope Asia never catches cold!)

In other words, Europe is a relatively small bulge on a much larger landmass. From a strictly geographical point of view, Europe is not a separate continent at all—it's part of Asia. But try telling that to the Europeans and Asians!

It's like two sisters who share a bedroom. To them, the room is clearly divided into separate parts. Each kid knows exactly which half is hers, which toys are hers, and which area she has to clean up. If one sister crosses the invisible dividing line, the other will surely tell Mom.

The same is true with Europe and Asia. You can't see a border. There's no ocean between them. Yet the Europeans and Asians know which part is theirs. And if one continent steps over the line, the other will run and tell Mom.

As you read in chapter 6, the Ural Mountains are the official border between Europe and Asia, yet the "real" border is cultural, not physical. It has changed over the centuries. Some people use religion as a dividing line—with Christian nations on the European side and Islamic nations on the Asian side.

But then, that doesn't explain Turkey. Until the end of the nineteenth

century, the whole southeast corner of Europe was ruled by the Islamic Turks. (Turkey was carved up in the early twentieth century. Greece, Albania, Hungary, Bulgaria, Rumania, Russia, and Yugoslavia all got slices of Turkey —sort of a territorial Thanksgiving.)

Russia is also confusing. It is the largest country on Earth . . . almost twice the size of Canada, the second largest country. The border between Europe and Asia cuts right through Russia from top to bottom.

Three-quarters of Russia is on the Asian side. That makes it Asian, right?

The capital (Moscow) and most of the people and cities are on the European side. That makes it European, right?

Then there's Iceland, an island nation in the North Atlantic. Iceland is part of Europe . . . even though it's right next to Greenland, which is part of North America.

What do all these oddities tell us? They show that geography is strongly linked to history. Deciding what country belongs on which continent depends not just on where it is but on who lives there, how they got there, and who's in charge of drawing the maps. It reminds us that geography is the study not only of places but of people.

The People

Remember the jungles of Africa and the rain forest in South America? Travel was difficult, and finding a taxi next to impossible. So tribes stayed home—and stayed separate.

In Europe, however, travel was relatively easy. The continent is small, as continents go. One tribe was always popping over to the tribe next door to borrow a cup of sugar. Trade flourished. The tribes soon banded together into what we now call nations.

Why? Well, for one thing, all that trade and travel meant that everyone was always minding everyone else's business.

For another thing, unity was more efficient. At one time, each city, each bank, and sometimes each nobleman produced its own money. This caused a lot of confusion in the shopping malls.

The people had two logical choices:

create nations and let them print the money, or forget about cash and use credit cards. Since plastic hadn't been invented yet, the Europeans decided to create nations.

Today, we can separate most of these nations into three major groups, depending on the languages they speak. The first group, clustered around the Mediterranean Sea in the south, speaks Romance languages. This does *not* mean that they're always telling each other how beautiful their eyes are or saying other romantic things. It means that their languages are based on Latin, the language of ancient Rome. French,

BEFORE MODERN EUROPEAN NATIONS WERE CREATED, SOMETIMES EACH NOBLEMAN PRODUCED HIS OWN MONEY!

YOU LIKE IT?

Spanish, Italian, Rumanian, and Portuguese are Romance languages.

The second group, ranged across the northwestern part of the continent,

ROMAN CE LANGUAGES

E PLURIBUS UNUM

speaks Germanic languages. This includes German, of course, as well as English, Dutch, Swedish, Norwegian, Danish, and Icelandic.

The third major group, in eastern and northeastern Europe, speaks Slavic languages, such as Russian, Polish, Bulgarian, Czechoslovakian, Serbo-Croatian, and Slovenian. In Eastern Europe, there are also people who speak languages that don't fit into any of these groups, including Hungarian, Turkish, Finnish, and Albanian. By and large, there are more languages—and they're more jumbled together—in the East than in the West.

Why? Imagine that you're in a room. If you sit near the door, you'll feel a breeze every time someone goes in or out. If you sit away from the door, you'll barely notice a thing.

Being in Eastern Europe, right next to the flat plains of Asia, was like being next to the door. But instead of a breeze blowing in, it was Turks, Hungarians, Mongols, and other Asian peoples. Populations were constantly being reshuffled.

As a result, much of Eastern Europe is a stew of different peoples, languages, and religions. This makes for lots of arguments about which land belongs to which country. National borders in Eastern Europe have changed more often than in the West and are still changing today.

This constant change can make things perplexing. Consider a family living in the city of Lvov for the last eighty years. Grandma would've been born in Austria, Mom in Poland, the kids in the Soviet Union, and the great-grandchildren in Ukraine—all without ever leaving Lvov.

Imagine how you'd feel if your hometown kept switching countries. Every time the government changed, your old money and postage stamps would be worthless. You'd always be learning new languages and new national anthems.

Western Europe, by contrast, has been relatively stable for ages. The borders of Spain, Portugal, France, Great Britain, Belgium, Denmark, Switzerland, Holland, and others are much the same now as they were two hundred years ago.

This may explain why it was mainly the Western European nations that set up colonies around the globe. Eastern Europeans were too busy arguing over their own countries to worry about getting a piece of somebody else's.

Water, Water Everywhere

Let's try an experiment. Walk across the room in a straight line and count how many steps it takes. Now walk across the room in a zigzag and count the steps.

The zigzag took more steps, right? You've just discovered one of the big secrets of Europe's success.

Europe's coast is zigzaggy. This means that even though Europe is small, its coast is long. In fact, Europe has a longer coastline than Africa . . . even though Africa is nearly three times bigger.

Many of the zigzags are peninsulas. A peninsula is a strip of land with water on three sides. A diving board jutting into a pool is like a peninsula, except peninsulas don't bounce.

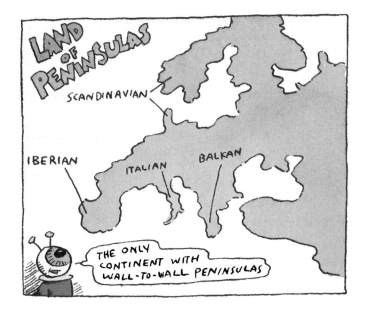

The Scandinavian, Iberian, and Balkan peninsulas are each big enough to hold several countries. Others are smaller. The Italian peninsula has just one country on it (which shares the same name) and is the easiest to find. It's shaped like a big boot and looks as if it's about to kick the island of Sicily for a field goal.

Of course, when you get right down to it, the continent of Europe itself is really just a big peninsula poking out of Asia.

Europe also has dozens of islands. There are little ones, including the Greek isles and the Isle of Man (but no Isle of Woman). And there are big ones, like Great Britain, Ireland, and Iceland. All of this adds up to a lot of beachfront property, with bays and harbors galore.

Compare that to what we learned about Africa a few chapters back. Africa has straight sides with few good ports. Merchants arriving at Africa had trouble getting in. Europe's coast, by comparison, is one big revolving door.

It was a well-used revolving door too. European history over the last five hundred years is very much a story of comings and goings. Traders trooped back and forth with shopping bags. Explorers went in and out searching for new markets. You already know about Columbus, who wanted to open a chain of Italian restaurants in China but bumped into the Americas on the way. Other European explorers included Ferdinand Magellan (whose ship

was the first to sail around the world), Vasco da Gama (who sailed from Europe, around Africa, to Asia), and Captain Cook (who found Australia . . . even though Australia wasn't missing).

European explorers were followed around the world by missionaries and merchants, who brought Christianity and commerce. Close on their heels came European settlers, who brought their families. More recently, Europeans have brought fancy bottled water, smelly cheese, and British television programs.

By the end of the nineteenth century, European settlers had spread across most of North and South America and Australia. In many other places—much of Asia and Africa—they controlled the economy. The only place left was Antarctica. And if they'd known any good recipes for penguin stew, Europeans might have moved there, too.

It is probably stretching things a bit to say that Europe's zigzaggy coast is responsible for all this activity. Good land, good weather, good natural resources, and good luck also helped make the continent strong.

But the fact is, sailing, settling, and selling went hand in hand. Just look at Venice (in the northeast corner of

Italy). Many great European cities were built near the water. Venice was built smack in the middle of it.

Venice is really a bunch of tiny islands connected by small bridges. Boats loaded with goods sailed right up the streets. Venice was like a giant drive-in supermarket.

And in a larger sense, all of Europe was like a drive-in supermarket, with dozens of rivers serving as the aisles between the well-stocked shelves.

The Volga (Europe's longest river) was vital to the growth of Russia. The Danube (which flows from Germany's *Black* Forest to the *Black* Sea, but somehow became known as the *blue* Danube) passes through eight countries and three national capitals.

Europe's busiest commercial waterway, the Rhine, starts in Switzerland, runs along Liechtenstein and France, cuts across Germany, and exits through the Netherlands to the North Sea.

Lots of coastline and lots of rivers may not be enough to ensure success. But if you think it's easy to become a great marketplace without waterways, you're all wet.

The Alps

Every continent has its ups and downs. In Europe, they're called "the Alps."

The snow-capped peaks of this mountain range are up; the green, wooded valleys are down. The tourists climb up, then they ski back down. Even Alpine singing is up and down. It's called yodeling and uses only high notes and low notes, with nothing in between.

The Alps are arranged in a 600-mile arc over the top of the boot-shaped Italian peninsula. Imagine that Europe is a huge face. The Alps would be its mouth, twisted into a big scowl.

EUROPE'S GREAT WATERWAYS WERE A BIG FACTOR IN HER SUCCESS

EURO-DUDE

GREAT WATERWAYS, MAN

The Alps are important to Europe's history, weather, and geography. They helped shape history by making it hard for outsiders to invade—which is how the Alpine country of Switzerland has managed to stay out of so many European fights.

As for weather, the Alps separate southern Europe from northern Europe. The people in the south were clustered around the warm Mediterranean Sea. The climate was mild enough for them to sit outside strumming guitars, until the neighbors shouted to knock it off.

The northerners, meanwhile, were exposed to chill Arctic winds. They knitted lots of heavy sweaters and fished the cold North Sea and Atlantic Ocean for herring and cod.

Though the Alps acted as a barrier, however, they didn't cut off *all* trade and communication. They were like the guard at the door of a nightclub, who keeps out enough people to make the place seem exclusive . . . but not so many that the place is empty.

The Alps are also important geographically as a birthplace of rivers. If you leave a mountain chain lying around in the rain, water will naturally run down the slopes, collect in the val-

leys, and flow off in all directions.

Today, the Alps are among the most built-up of the world's major mountain ranges, with big cities and lots of vacation resorts. One reason the Alps are so well developed is that they are full of good roads. You don't have to tie a rope around your waist to get from one hotel to another.

Many of these roads were left behind two hundred years ago by the French emperor Napoleon. He built them to get his army across the mountains on its way to conquering the rest of Europe. Now the rest of Europe uses the roads to conquer the Alps.

Nature

Most of Europe's plants and animals are cultivated.

That doesn't mean European shrubbery goes to the opera every night, or that European chickens sip tea with their pinkies sticking out. It means that they are bred and grown by people, rather than left to do their own thing. There's little truly remote wilderness left in Europe.

Why? First, Europe is a small place crowded with lots of people. They've spent centuries clearing land, planting petunias, building fences,

FEELS LIKE I'VE BEEN CLEARING THIS LAND FOR CENTURIES

and mowing lawns. Second, as we've already discussed, Europe is lucky enough to have good soil and pretty decent weather—just right for farming.

On other continents, vast deserts, rain forests, or dry grasslands kept most people away from certain parts. You couldn't plant rhubarb and zucchini there if you wanted to (and plenty of folks wouldn't want to). In Europe, there were acres of good land . . . so Europeans built acres of farms.

Europe was also tamed by the Industrial Revolution. That was the era, which started about two hundred years ago, when people began inventing and building all sorts of machines that were fast, efficient, and didn't call in sick on Friday mornings. Europeans began covering the continent with steam engines and trains, mills and mines, factories and roads.

The result of all this human activity shows up today in Europe's plants and animals. Many of the leading crops are not native. Wheat, barley, olives, flax, grapes, figs, peppers, tomatoes, potatoes, peaches, rice, oats—all are important in Europe, and all were brought from other continents.

As for animals, thousands of years of

breeding have left their mark. Most of the continent's big game animals are gone. For instance, the aurochs, the wild ox of Europe, has been extinct for over 350 years. *Extinct* means that the last aurochs died without leaving any little aurochses. But you probably know its great-great-granddaughter: the cow.

Some wild animals survive, of course. There are still wolves and boars, badgers and polecats. But even the wild animals somehow don't seem all that wild. You're more likely to see a brown bear performing in a circus than trotting through the woods. You don't hear much about foxes unless they're being chased by well-dressed English ladies and gentlemen.

Europe is a beautiful continent, mind you, with twittering birds, dramatic scenery, and enough flowers to keep allergy sufferers sneezing away all spring. It's just that there are so many signs of human influence all around. You often have the feeling that everything has been planned—that the flowers were planted by gardeners and the birds are on salary.

The major exception is the Far North, where it's too cold for farming, and where the frigid plains and forests are largely intact. Enormous herds of reindeer still wander back and forth across the Arctic lands.

The reindeer are probably pretty safe up there. After all, most folks wouldn't want to settle in that icy, barren land. There are rumors that a fat, jolly, bearded old guy in a red suit lives up there near the North Pole. But don't worry. He won't bother the reindeer . . . except maybe once a year.

People are always remarking that "it's a small world." And they're right. Distant regions of Earth—and the people who live in those regions—have a lot in common with one another.

Americans, Europeans, and Chinese used their rivers as highways. Africans and South Americans live in places where travel is difficult, and both continents are filled with separate groups speaking different languages. Native Americans and Australian aborigines shared similar experiences with the arrival of European colonists. And scientists in Antarctica have a lot in common with hockey players in Canada (both spend a lot of time on the ice).

At the same time, it's a "big world" as well. There are tremendous, fascinating differences between far-flung peoples and places. In Africa's Sahara, nomads crisscross the desert in search of water. In South America's Amazon, meanwhile, people slosh through the rain forest in search of galoshes.

Studying geography helps us discover how it's a "big small world"—how the land around us gives us much in common and much that's unique. Geography shapes lives, history, and traditions. If you want to understand what on Earth is going on, you've got to know *where* on Earth it's going on.

agriculture the practice and science of growing crops and raising livestock.

axis an imaginary line through the Earth around which the planet rotates; it runs from the North Pole to the South Pole.

canopy a network of treetops forming a dense, leafy ceiling over a forest, particularly a RAIN FOREST.

climate the typical weather of a place.

continent one of the main landmasses of Earth.

continental divide an area which divides the rivers flowing across a CONTINENT toward one ocean from those flowing in the other direction to a different ocean.

continental drift the constant movement of the CONTINENTS across the Earth's surface.

desert a region that receives an average of less than 10 inches of rain or snow a year.

equator an imaginary circle around the middle of the Earth that is everywhere the same distance from the North and South Poles.

fault a crack in the Earth's crust where two PLATES meet and often bump or rub against each other.

fossil the hardened remains of long-dead plants or animals.

glacier a huge mass of ice moving slowly down a slope or across a wide area of land.

harbor a body of water along the shore that is sheltered from wind and waves and deep enough for anchoring a ship.

hemisphere half of a ball or globe. Earth is divided across the middle into the Northern and Southern Hemispheres, and from top to bottom into the Eastern and Western Hemispheres.

icecap a permanent blanket of ice and snow, particularly the thick ice around the North and South Poles.

International Date Line an imaginary line drawn down the Pacific Ocean to separate one day from the next.

isthmus a skinny strip of land, bordered on both sides by water, connecting two larger bodies of land.

oasis a place in the desert where there is water.

ozone layer a blanket of ozone (a form of oxygen) high above the Earth that helps block harmful ultraviolet rays from the sun.

pampas the flat, grassy plains of southern South America.

peninsula a strip of land extending out into a body of water.

plates tremendous, slow-moving slabs of rocks that form the Earth's crust and carry the world's CONTINENTS and oceans.

plate tectonics the process which builds and shapes the Earth through the moving and bumping of the planet's PLATES.

rain forest a lush, wet, generally warm forest where rainfall averages at least 80 inches a year.

savanna a tropical or subtropical plain with enough rain in some seasons to grow grass, but not enough to grow many trees or dense woods.

steppe a vast, treeless plain, particularly the flat stretch of land south of Siberia.

strait a narrow passage of water connecting two large bodies of water.

subcontinent a large landmass forming a subdivision of a CONTINENT.

tributary a river or stream that flows into a larger river or other body of water.